"This is an illuminating and insightful tour of financial statements, how they can be used to inform, how they can be used to mislead, and how they can be used to analyze the financial health of a company."
    —Jay O. Light, Dean Emeritus, Harvard Business School

"*Financial Statement Analysis* should be required reading for anyone who puts a dime to work in the securities markets or recommends that others do the same."
    —Jack L. Rivkin, Director, Neuberger Berman Mutual Funds and Idealab

"Fridson and Alvarez provide a valuable practical guide for understanding, interpreting, and critically assessing financial reports put out by firms. Their discussion of profits—'quality of earnings'—is particularly insightful given the recent spate of reporting problems encountered by firms. I highly recommend their book to anyone interested in getting behind the numbers as a means of predicting future profits and stock prices."
    —Paul Brown, Associate Dean, Executive MBA Programs,
    Leonard N. Stern School of Business, New York University

"Let this book assist in financial awareness and transparency and higher standards of reporting, and accountability to all stakeholders."
    —Patricia A. Small, Treasurer Emeritus, University of California;
    Partner, KCM Investment Advisors

"This book is a polished gem covering the analysis of financial statements. It is thorough, skeptical, and extremely practical in its review."
    —Daniel J. Fuss, Vice Chairman, Loomis, Sayles & Company, LP

Financial Statement Analysis Workbook

Financial Statement Analysis Workbook

Step-by-Step Exercises and Tests to Help You Master Financial Statement Analysis

Fourth Edition

MARTIN FRIDSON
FERNANDO ALVAREZ

John Wiley & Sons, Inc.

For general information on our other products and services or for technical support, please contact our Customer Care Department within the United States at (800) 762-2974, outside the United States at (317) 572-3993 or fax (317) 572-4002.

Wiley also publishes its books in a variety of electronic formats. Some content that appears in print may not be available in electronic books. For more information about Wiley products, visit our web site at www.wiley.com.

ISBN 978-0-470-64003-6 (paperback); ISBN 978-1-118-09749-6 (ebk);
ISBN 978-1-118-09747-2 (ebk); ISBN 978-1-118-09748-9 (ebk)

10 9 8 7 6 5 4 3 2 1

In memory of my father, Harry Yale Fridson, who introduced me to accounting, economics, and logic, as well as the fourth discipline essential to the creation of this book—hard work!
M. F.

For Shari, Virginia, and Armando.
F. A.

Contents

Preface to Fourth Edition Workbook

This fourth edition of *Financial Statement Analysis,* like its predecessors, seeks to equip its readers for practical challenges of contemporary business. Once again, the intention is to acquaint readers who have already acquired basic accounting skills with the complications that arise in applying textbook-derived knowledge to the real world of extending credit and investing in securities. Just as a swiftly changing environment necessitated extensive revisions and additions in the second edition, new concerns and challenges for users of financial statements have accompanied the dawn of the twenty-first century.

For one thing, corporations have shifted their executive compensation plans increasingly toward rewarding senior managers for "enhancing shareholder value." This lofty-sounding concept has a dark side. Chief executive officers who are under growing pressure to boost their corporations' share prices can no longer increase their bonuses by goosing reported earnings through financial reporting tricks that are transparent to the stock market. They must instead devise more insidious methods that gull investors into believing that the reported earnings gains are real. In response to this trend, we have expanded our survey of revenue recognition gimmicks designed to deceive the unwary.

Another innovation that demands increased vigilance by financial analysts is the conversion of stock market proceeds into revenues. In terms of accounting theory, this kind of transformation is the equivalent of alchemy. Companies generate revenue by selling goods or services, not by selling their own shares to the public.

During the Internet stock boom of the late 1990s, however, clever operators found a way around that constraint. Companies took the money they raised in initial public offerings, bought advertising on one another's web sites, and recorded the shuttling of dollars as sales. Customers were superfluous to the revenue recognition process. In another variation on the theme, franchisers sold stock, lent the proceeds to franchisees, then immediately had the cash returned under the rubric of fees. By going out for a short stroll and coming back, the proceeds of a financing mutated into revenues.

The artificial nature of these revenues becomes apparent when readers combine an understanding of accounting principles with a corporate finance perspective. We facilitate such integration of disciplines throughout *Financial Statement Analysis,* making excursions into economics and business management as well. In addition, we encourage analysts to consider the institutional context in which financial reporting occurs. Organizational pressures result in divergences from elegant theories, both in the conduct of financial statement analysis and in auditors' interpretations of accounting principles. The issuers of financial statements also exert a strong influence over the creation of the financial principles, with powerful politicians sometimes carrying their water.

A final area in which the new edition offers a sharpened focus involves success stories in the critical examination of financial statements. Wherever we can find the necessary documentation, we show not only how a corporate debacle *could have been* foreseen through application of basis analytical techniques, but also how practicing analysts actually did detect the problem before it became widely recognized. Readers will be encouraged by these examples, we hope, to undertake genuine, goal-oriented analysis, instead of simply going through the motions of calculating standard financial ratios. Moreover, the case studies should persuade them to stick to their guns when they spot trouble, despite management's predictable litany. ("Our financial statements are consistent with generally accepted accounting principles. They have been certified by one of the world's premier auditing firms. We will not allow a band of greedy short-sellers to destroy the value created by our outstanding employees.") Typically, as the vehemence of management's protests increases, conditions deteriorate and accusations of aggressive accounting give way to revelations of fraudulent financial reporting.

The principles and theories put forth in the University Edition of *Financial Statement Analysis,* fourth edition, are reinforced through the questions and exercises in this workbook. Part One, Questions, provides chapter-by-chapter fill-in-the-blank questions, financial statement exercises, and computational exercises. They are designed to be thought-provoking exercises requiring analysis and synthesis of the concepts covered in the book. In short, these questions do not call for "regurgitation of information."

The answers to all questions can be found in Part Two. Answers are provided in ***boldfaced, italic type*** in order to facilitate the checking of answers and comprehension of the material.

Financial markets continue to evolve, but certain phenomena appear again and again in new guises. In this vein, companies never lose their resourcefulness in finding new ways to skew perceptions of their performance. By studying their methods closely, analysts can potentially anticipate the variations on old themes that will materialize in years to come.

MARTIN FRIDSON
FERNANDO ALVAREZ

Acknowledgments

Mukesh Agarwal
John Bace
Mimi Barker
Mitchell Bartlett
Richard Bernstein
Richard Byrne
Richard Cagney
George Chalhoub
Tiffany Charbonier
Sanford Cohen
Margarita Declet
Mark Dunham
Kenneth Emery
Bill Falloon
Sylvan Feldstein
David Fitton
Thomas Flynn III
Daniel Fridson
Igor Fuksman
Ryan Gelrod
Kenneth Goldberg
Susannah Gray
Evelyn Harris
David Hawkins
Emilie Herman
Avi Katz
Rebecca Keim
James Kenney
Andrew Kroll
Les Levi
Ross Levy
Michael Lisk
David Lugg
Jennie Ma

Stan Manoukian
Michael Marocco
Tom Marshella
Eric Matejevich
John Mattis
Pat McConnell
Oleg Melentyev
Krishna Memani
Ann Marie Mullan
Kingman Penniman
Stacey Rivera
Richard Rolnick
Clare Schiedermayer
Gary Schieneman
Bruce Schwartz
Devin Scott
David Shapiro
Elaine Sisman
Charles Snow
Vladimir Stadnyk
John Thieroff
Scott Thomas
John Tinker
Kivin Varghese
Diane Vazza
Pamela Van Giessen
Sharyl Van Winkle
David Waill
Steven Waite
Douglas Watson
Burton Weinstein
Stephen Weiss
David Whitcomb
Mark Zand

One

Questions

Questions on Each Chapter

CHAPTER 1: THE ADVERSARIAL NATURE OF FINANCIAL REPORTING

1. Three ways that corporations can use financial reporting to enhance their value are:
   a. _____
   b. _____
   c. _____
2. The true purpose of financial reporting is _____.
3. Corporations routinely _____ because the appearance of _____ receives a higher _____ multiple.
4. According to the _____, reversals of the excess write-offs offer an artificial means of _____ in subsequent periods.
5. The following are some of the powerful limitations to continued growth faced by companies:
   a. _____
   b. _____
   c. _____
6. Some of the commonly heard rationalizations for declining growth are:
   a. _____
   b. _____
   c. _____
7. _____ reached its zenith of popularity during the _____ movement of the 1960s. However, by the 1980s, the stock market had converted the _____ into a _____.
8. _____ is one of the ways that the notion of diversification as a means of maintaining _____ is revived from time to time.

9. The surprise element in Manville Corporation's 1982 bankruptcy was, in part, a function of _____.

10. The analyst's heightened awareness of legal risks are a result of bankruptcies associated with:

    a. _____

    b. _____

    c. _____

11. Some of the stories used to sell stocks to individual investors are:

    a. _____

    b. A "play" in some current economic trend such as

        i. _____

        ii. _____

    c. _____

12. When the story used to sell stocks to individual investors originates among stockbrokers or even _____, the zeal with which the story is disseminated may depend more on _____ than the _____.

13. The ostensible purpose of financial reporting is _____ of a corporation's earnings.

14. Over a two-year period BGT paid L&H $35 million to develop translation software. L&H then bought BGT and the translation product along with it. The net effect was that instead _____, L&H recognized _____.

CHAPTER 2: THE BALANCE SHEET

1. A study conducted on behalf of Big Five accounting firm Arthur Andersen showed that between _____ and _____, book value fell from _____ percent to _____ percent of the stock market value of public companies in the United States.

2. As noted by Baruch Lev of New York University, two examples of how traditional accounting systems are at a loss to capture most of what is going on today are:

    a. _____

    b. _____

3. In the examples in Question 2 there is no accounting event because
_____.

4. Some of the distinct approaches that have evolved for assessing real property are:
   a. _____
   b. _____
   c. _____

5. Some financial assets are unaffected by the difficulties of evaluating physical assets because _____ in _____ markets.

6. Under the compromise embodied in SFAS 115, financial instruments are valued according to _____ by the company_____.

7. If a company wrote off a billion dollars worth of goodwill, its ratio of assets to liabilities would _____. Its ratio of _____ would not change, however.

8. Through stock-for-stock acquisitions, the sharp rise in equity prices during the late 1990s was transformed into _____, despite the usual assumption that _____.

9. Unlike _____, goodwill is not an asset that can be readily _____ to raise cash. Neither can a company enter into a _____ of its goodwill, as it can with its plant and equipment. In short, goodwill is not _____ that management can either _____ or _____ to extricate itself from a financial tight spot.

10. A reasonable estimate of a low-profit company's true equity value would be _____.

11. Determining the cost of capital is a notoriously controversial subject in the financial field, complicated by _____ and _____.

12. Among the advantages of market capitalization as a measure of equity are:
    a. _____
    b. _____
    c. _____

13. A limitation of the peer-group approach to valuation is that _____ and therefore _____ one major benefit of using _____ as a gauge of actual equity value.

14. Instead of striving for theoretical purity on the matter, analysts should adopt a ＿＿＿＿＿＿＿＿＿, using the measure of equity value ＿＿＿＿＿＿＿＿＿.

15. Historical-cost-based balance sheet figures are the ones that matter in ＿＿＿＿＿＿＿＿ that a company will violate ＿＿＿＿＿＿＿＿＿ requiring ＿＿＿＿＿＿＿＿＿.

16. Users of financial statements can process only ＿＿＿＿＿＿＿＿＿, and they do not always have ＿＿＿＿＿＿＿＿＿.

17. Deterioration in a company's financial position may catch investors by surprise because it ＿＿＿＿＿＿＿＿ and is ＿＿＿＿＿＿＿＿＿.

CHAPTER 3: THE INCOME STATEMENT

1. Students of financial statements must keep up with ＿＿＿＿＿＿＿＿＿ of the past few years in transforming ＿＿＿＿＿＿＿＿ into ＿＿＿＿＿＿＿＿＿.

2. In the ＿＿＿＿＿＿＿＿＿, each income statement item is expressed as ＿＿＿＿＿＿＿＿ (sales or revenues), which is represented as ＿＿＿＿＿＿＿＿＿.

3. Besides facilitating comparisons between a company's present and past results, the ＿＿＿＿＿＿＿＿ can highlight important facts ＿＿＿＿＿＿＿＿＿.

4. Even within an industry, the breakdown of expenses can vary from company to company as a function of ＿＿＿＿＿＿＿＿ and ＿＿＿＿＿＿＿＿＿.

5. Percentage breakdowns are also helpful for comparing a single company's performance with ＿＿＿＿＿＿＿＿ and for comparing ＿＿＿＿＿＿＿＿ on the basis of ＿＿＿＿＿＿＿＿.

6. In essence, Peet's is more of ＿＿＿＿＿＿＿＿ and Starbucks is more involved in ＿＿＿＿＿＿＿＿.

7. Costs as percentages of sales also vary among companies within an industry for ＿＿＿＿＿＿＿＿ than differences ＿＿＿＿＿＿＿＿.

8. The more widely diversified pharmaceutical manufacturers can be expected to have ＿＿＿＿＿＿＿＿ percentage ＿＿＿＿＿＿＿＿, as well as ＿＿＿＿＿＿＿＿ percentage expenses, than industry peers that focus exclusively on ＿＿＿＿＿＿＿＿.

9. Analysts must take care not to mistake difference that is actually _____ as evidence of _____. A subtler explanation may be available at the modest cost of _____.

10. Executives whose bonuses rise _____ have a strong incentive not only _____, but also to use _____.

11. On a retrospective basis, a surge _____ or _____ may indicate that _____.

12. Along with _____, another major expense category that can be controlled through _____ is _____.

13. An unusually low ratio of _____ to _____ with the ratios of its industry peers may indicate that management is being unrealistic in acknowledging the pace of wear and tear on fixed assets. Understatement of _____ and overstatement of _____ would result.

14. A company knows that creating _____ expectations about _____ can raise _____ and lower _____.

15. One way persuading investors that a major development that hurt earnings last year will _____ affect earnings _____ is to suggest that any _____ suffered by the company was somehow _____, and, by implication, _____.

16. An extraordinary item is reported on an _____ basis, below the _____ from continuing operations.

17. The accounting rules prohibit corporate officials from displaying certain hits to earnings "above the line," that is, _____, and from using the label _____. Accordingly they employ designations such as _____ or _____. These terms have _____, but _____ the highlighted items are _____.

18. In recent years, _____ has become a catchall for charges that companies wish analysts to consider _____, but which do not qualify for _____.

19. Corporate managers commonly perceive that _____ will be _____ if they take (for sake of argument) a $1.5 billion write-off than if _____. The benefit of exaggerating the damage is that in subsequent years, _____.

20. The most dangerous trap that users of financial statements must avoid walking into, however, is inferring that the term "restructuring" connotes _____.

21. The purpose of providing pro forma results was to help analysts _____ accurately when some event _____ caused _____ to convey a misleading impression.

22. Computer software producers got into the act by _____ from the expenses considered in calculating _____.

23. Unlike operating income, a concept addressed by FASB standards, _____ is a number that subjectively _____ many _____ that lack any standing under GAAP.

24. In fact, analysts who hope to forecast future financial results accurately *must* apply _____ and set aside genuinely _____.

25. Analysts must exercise judgment when considering pro forma earnings; however, they must make sure to examine _____, instead of _____ by relying solely on _____.

26. An older, but not obsolete, device for beefing up reported income is _____.

27. A comparatively _____ ratio of PP&E to _____ or _____ is another sign of potential trouble.

28. Management can _____ through techniques that more properly fall into the category of _____.

29. One way to increase profitability through _____ involves _____.

30. A corporation can easily accelerate its sales growth by _____ and _____. Creating genuine value for shareholders through _____ is more difficult, although unwary investors sometimes fail to recognize the distinction.

31. Analysts need to distinguish between internal growth and external growth. _____ consists of sales increases generated from a company's existing operations, while _____ represents incremental sales brought in through _____.

32. If Company A generates external growth by acquiring Company B and neither Company nor its new subsidiary increases its profitability, then _____ the merged companies is _____ than the sum of the two companies' values.

33. In general, the _____ the combining businesses are, the _____ it is that the hoped-for economies of scope _____.

34. As synergies go, projections of economies of scale in combinations of companies _____ tend to be more plausible than economies of scope purportedly available to companies in _____ businesses.

35. A company with relatively large _____ has a _____ breakeven level. Even a modest economic downturn will reduce _____ below the rate required to keep the company profitable.

36. Deals that work on paper have often foundered on
    a. _____
    b. _____
    c. _____
    d. _____

37. Financial statements cannot capture certain _____ that may be essential to _____. These include
    a. _____
    b. _____
    c. _____

CHAPTER 4: THE STATEMENT OF CASH FLOWS

1. The present version of the statement that traces the flow of funds in and out of the firm, the statement of cash flows, became mandatory, under _____, for issuers with fiscal years ending after _____.

2. For financial-reporting (as opposed to _____) purposes, a publicly owned company generally seeks to maximize _____, which investors use as a basis for valuing its shares.

3. A privately held company, unlike a _____, which shows one set of statements to the public and another to the Internal Revenue Service, a private company typically prepares _____ of statements, with _____ foremost in its thinking. Its incentive is

not _____, but to _____, the income it reports, thereby _____ its tax bill as well.

4. In a classic LBO, a group of investors acquires a business by _____ and _____ the balance.

5. The amount attributable to depreciation _____ in the current year. Rather, it is a bookkeeping entry intended to represent the _____, through use, _____.

6. Viewed in terms of cash inflows and outflows, rather than earnings, _____ begins to look like _____.

7. Analysts evaluating the investment merits of the LBO proposal would miss the point if they focused on _____ rather than _____.

8. In an LBO, the equity investors do not reap spectacular gains without incurring significant _____. There is a danger that everything _____ and that they will lose _____. Specifically, there is a risk that _____ will fall short of expectations, perhaps as a result of _____ or because the investors' expectations _____.

9. The _____, rather than the _____, provides the best information about a highly leveraged firm's financial health.

10. Among the applications and uses of the Statement of Cash Flows are:
    a. _____
    b. _____
    c. _____

11. When a company is _____, its balance sheet may _____ its asset value, as a result of _____ having lagged the _____ of the company's operations.

12. Revenues build gradually during the _____ phase, during which time the company is just _____ and _____.

13. Growth and profits accelerate rapidly during the _____ phase, as the company's products begin to penetrate the market and the _____.

14. During the _____ period, growth in sales and earnings decelerates as the _____. In the _____ phase, sales opportunities are limited to the replacement of products previously sold, plus _____.

15. Price competition often intensifies at this stage, as companies _____. The _____ stage does not automatically follow maturity, but over long periods some industries do get swept away by _____.

16. Sharply declining sales and earnings, ultimately resulting in _____, characterize industries in decline.

17. _____ are typically voracious cash users.

18. _____ are start-ups that survive long enough to reach the stage of entering the public market.

19. For a company at _____, it may take several years for sales to reach _____ sizable fixed costs that are _____.

20. Unlike a _____, Green Mountain is _____. It issues substantial _____ each year to fund its _____.

21. _____ are in a less precarious state in terms of cash flow than their emerging growth counterparts.

22. Reflecting the _____ of its business, Kimberly-Clark generates a _____ level of _____.

23. Far from depending _____, this mature company _____, giving them the opportunity to _____ it in higher-growth, _____.

24. Some _____ choose instead to _____ internally. They either launch or acquire businesses with _____. The older businesses become _____ for funding the newer activities.

25. _____ are past the cash strain faced by growth companies that must fund large _____ programs.

26. _____ struggle to generate sufficient cash as a consequence of meager earnings.

27. By studying the cash flow statement, an analyst can make informed judgments on such questions as:

    a. _____

    b. _____

    c. _____

28. In difficult times, when a company must cut back on various expenditures _____, management faces many difficult choices. A key objective is to _____.

29. At times, _____ becomes _____, as a function _____ or _____. During the _____ that occasionally befall the business world, _____ is unavailable at any price.

30. If a corporation's financial strain becomes acute, the board of directors may take the comparatively extreme step of _____.

31. Reducing _____ is a step that corporations try very hard to avoid, for fear of _____ and consequently suffering an increase in _____.

32. A final factor in assessing financial flexibility is the change in adjusted working capital. Unlike conventional working capital _____, this figure excludes _____, as well as _____ and _____.

33. A company with a strong balance sheet can fund much of that cash need by increasing its _____ (credit extended by vendors). External financing may be needed, however, if accumulation of unsold goods causes _____ to rise disproportionately to _____. Similarly, if customers begin paying more slowly than formerly, can widen the gap between _____ and _____.

34. One typical consequence of violating _____ or striving to head off _____ is that management reduces discretionary expenditures to avoid _____.

35. Overinvestment has unquestionably led, in many industries, to prolonged periods of _____, producing in turn chronically _____. In retrospect, the firms involved would have served their shareholders better if they had _____ or _____, instead of _____.

36. Keeping cash "trapped" in marketable securities can enable a firm _____ over "lean-and-mean" competitors when _____ make it difficult to _____.

37. Another less obvious risk of eschewing financial flexibility is the danger of permanently losing _____ through _____ occasioned by recessions.

38. The income statement is a dubious measure of the success of a _____ company that is being managed to _____ rather than _____, reported profits.

39. The cash flow statement is the best tool for measuring _____, which, contrary to a widely held view, is not merely a security blanket for _____.

40. In the hands of an aggressive but prudent management, a cash flow cushion can enable a company to _____ when competitors are forced to cut back.

CHAPTER 5: WHAT IS PROFIT?

1. Profitability is a yardstick by which businesspeople can measure their _____ and justify _____.

2. When calculating _____ profits, the analyst must take care to consider only genuine revenues and deduct all relevant costs.

3. There can be no bona fide profit without _____. Bona fide profits are the only kind of profits _____ in financial analysis.

4. Merely _____, it is clear, does not increase wealth.

5. An essential element of genuinely useful financial statement analysis is: _____.

6. The issuer of the statements can _____ or _____ its reported earnings simply by using its latitude to assume shorter or longer _____.

7. The rate at which the tax code allows owners to write off property overstates _____.

8. In the _____, companies typically record depreciation and amortization expense that far exceeds physical wear-and-tear on assets.

9. In many industries, fixed assets consist mainly of _____. The major risk of analytical error does not arise from the possibility that _____, but the reverse.

CHAPTER 6: REVENUE RECOGNITION

1. Many corporations employ _____ practices that comply with GAAP yet _____.

2. Under intense pressure to maintain their stock prices, companies characterized by _____ seem particularly prone _____.

3. To seasoned investors, _____ by a senior manager represents _____.

4. Bonus-seeking managers may initially veer off the straight-and-narrow by _____ a small amount from _____, intending to _____ the following year, but they instead fall further and further behind. Eventually, the gap between _____ and _____ grows too large to sustain.

5. Even when an independent accounting firm certifies that a company's financials _____ with generally accepted accounting principles; the analyst must stay alert for evidence _____.

6. Staying alert to evidence of flawed, _____, reporting is essential, even when the auditors _____.

7. As a rule, distorting one section of the financial statements _____. Assiduous tracking of a variety of _____ should raise serious questions about a company's reporting, at a minimum.

8. The explanation for the sudden drop in projected earnings was that in 2001 Bristol-Myers _____ to induce them to _____ at a much faster rate than necessary to _____.

9. "_____" is a security analysts' term for the financial reporting gimmick that Bristol-Myers employed _____.

10. Along with other pharmaceutical producers, Bristol-Myers was feeling profit pressures due to _____ to replace sales of products _____.

11. Haydon was known for speaking candidly about Bristol-Myers's declining sales prospects. Consequently, his reassignment was _____.

12. Also suspect was Bristol-Myers's repeated practice of _____ that exactly equaled _____.

13. The Bristol-Myers Squibb case study nevertheless illustrates the value of _____ against _____.

14. According to Take-Two management, the adjustment arose because the company _____ on some games it sold to "_____" but which were later _____ by Take-Two.

15. _____ to the lesson taught by many other cases of financial misreporting, it paid to accept the Take-Two _____ assurances that the company's business prospects _____.

16. Take-Two shipped hundreds of thousands of video games to distributors _____, _____ booked the shipments _____, then _____ in later periods.

17. Encouragingly for users of financial statements, managers _____ are often betrayed by _____.

18. In layaway sales, customers reserve goods _____, and then make additional payments over a specified period, _____ when they have paid in full.

19. Prior to the change in accounting practice, which FAS 101 made mandatory, Wal-Mart booked layaway sales _____. Under the new and more conservative method, the company began to recognize the sales _____.

20. On the whole, Bally's reported profit margins benefited from the increase in _____ as a percentage of total revenues. The reported earnings, however, rested on assumptions regarding the percentage of customers who _____.

21. As in any sales situation, aggressive pursuit of new business could result in _____. On average, the newer members might prove to be _____ or less committed to physical fitness than _____.

22. There was no change in the accounting principle, namely _____. In the case of a health club, members' upfront fees represent _____. Club operators should therefore recognize the revenue over the period in which _____.

23. Under GAAP, the general requirement was to spread membership fees _____. If a company offered refunds, it could not _____ until the refund period expired, unless there was _____ to enable management to _____ estimate _____ with reasonable confidence.

24. Under certain circumstances, a company engaged in long-term contract work can _____. This result arises from GAAP's solution to a mismatch commonly observed _____.

25. GAAP addresses the problem through the _____, which permits the company to recognize revenue in _____, rather than in line with its billing.

26. As is generally the case with _____, taking liberties with the percentage-of-completion borrows _____, making a surprise _____ at some point.

27. The SEC claimed that management at Sequoia Systems inflated revenue and profits by:

   a. _____

   b. _____

   c. _____

28. The SEC also claimed that management at Sequoia Systems profited from the scheme by _____.

29. Loading the distribution channels consists of _____ to accept larger shipments of goods than _____.

30. Loading does not boost _____, but merely shifts the timing of its _____.

31. Inevitably, the underlying trend of final sales to consumers slows down, at least temporarily. At that point, the manufacturer's growth in reported revenue will maintain its trend only _____, relative to their sales. If the distributors balk, _____, forcing a _____, of previously recorded profits.

32. Krispy Kreme revised its senior executive compensation plan.[1] Henceforth, officers would receive _____ unless the company _____ in each quarter _____.

33. In essence, according to the *Wall Street Journal*'s story, Krispy Kreme _____ by taking money _____.

34. Had Krispy Kreme instead _____, it would have _____. The catch is that an asset is supposed to be _____. Terminated stores would not seem _____.

35. Most, if not all, of the _____ on Krispy Kreme's _____ appeared to have come from a _____ transaction, rather than from _____.

---

[1] *SEC v. Scott A. Livengood, John W. Tate, and Randy S. Casstevens. SEC Complaint against Scott A. Livengood, John W. Tate, and Randy S. Casstevens*, May 4, 2009.

36. Krispy Kreme increased the size of the corrections to its fiscal 2004 results. The previously undisclosed problems involved _____, _____, and _____.

37. Krispy Kreme was _____ fictitious earnings. Rather, the SEC complaint depicted a _____, through a wide range of _____, to beat _____.

38. An exceptionally long record of _____ or _____ is a reason to _____.

39. A second lesson of the Krispy Kreme case is that _____ and _____ often go hand in hand.

40. It is impossible to assess the quality of an internal investigation without information on the _____, and the basis _____.

41. Users of financial statements should not be intimidated by corporate _____ that denounce allegedly irresponsible _____.

42. In 2001, Halliburton adopted an even more aggressive approach to _____. For some projects, Halliburton began reporting sales _____. Previously, the policy was to book revenues _____. In addition, the company began keeping some disputed bills on the books _____. The previous policy was to refrain from a write-off only _____.

43. Halliburton became more aggressive about _____, a classic technique for _____.

44. If earnings look suspiciously _____ during a _____ for the company's industry, users of financial statements should _____ explains the disparity.

45. A stock's value is a function of expected _____, which partly depend on the _____ vis-à-vis its competitors'.

46. Generally, the initial response of corporate executives caught in a lie is _____, but gratifyingly often, _____.

47. Analysts who strive to go beyond routine _____ can profit by seeking _____ of corporate disclosure, even when _____ have already placed _____.

48. Sometimes, management _____ revenue recognition in order to _____ short-run profits. The motive for this paradoxical

behavior is a desire to report the sort of _____ that equity investors reward with _____.

49. Grace executives reckoned that with earnings already meeting Wall Street analysts' forecasts, a windfall _____ the company's stock price. Such an inference would have been consistent with investors' customary _____ that they perceive to be generated by _____.

50. Grace's 1998 statement that its auditors had raised no objections to its accounting for the Medicare reimbursement windfall was true only _____ that Price Waterhouse issued clean financials, based on materiality considerations. As a spokeswoman for the auditing firm pointed out, such an opinion _____.

51. According to Michael Jensen: "Tell a manager that he will get a bonus when targets are realized and two things will happen":
    a. _____
    b. _____

52. All too often, companies wouldn't be able to accomplish the frauds without _____.

53. According to Jensen, almost every company uses a budget system that _____ employees for _____ and punishes them _____. He proposes reforming the system by severing the link between _____ and _____.

54. Even in the case of the bluest of the blue chips, watching for rising levels of _____ or _____, relative to _____, should be standard operating procedure.

55. When the revenues derived from _____ fail to materialize, the managers may resort to _____. The positive mental attitude that overstates revenues in the early stage_____, however, than _____ at a later point.

CHAPTER 7: EXPENSE RECOGNITION

1. Corporate managers are just as creative _____ and _____ the recognition of as they are in maximizing and speeding up _____.

2. Investors attach little significance to _____ profits and losses in valuing stocks. Therefore, a public company has a strong incentive to _____ into a one-time event and to _____ nonrecurring into smaller pieces and _____.

3. Nortel Networks illustrated _____, one of the most _____ of financial reporting.

4. Between September 2000 and _____ Nortel's market capitalization sank *by* 99%, devastating _____ that were heavily invested in its shares.

5. The company had to wave a _____ with respect to _____ by _____ financial reports.

6. In addition to dashing hopes _____, Nortel rattled the market by firing _____ Dunn, _____ Beatty, and _____ Gollogly.

7. Nortel's management's credibility _____ as the _____ for producing definitive _____.

8. Nortel's investigation, which previously had focused on _____ had turned to _____.

9. Incorrect recognition of that amount resulted from a combination of:
   a. _____
   b. _____
   c. _____
   d. _____

10. Nortel followed a strategy of _____ in its money-losing period of 2001–2002. _____ created _____ that could be taken _____.

11. Nortel's experience shows that if a company _____, it will have no compunction about _____ through _____.

12. An important takeaway from the Nortel case is that _____ can prove _____.

13. _____ are another frequently abused element of _____. General Motors's fiddling with this device _____ in the *integrity* of financial reporting.

14. At issue in GM's restatement was _____ and _____ from _____.

15. GM said that some cash flows from _____ that should have been classified among its _____ were instead booked as _____.

16. This revelation puzzled accounting experts because the applicable rules were unambiguous. _____ or _____ fell into _____; _____ were included in _____.

17. GM Management said it had _____ it was leasing to car-rental companies, assuming they would be _____ more after those companies _____.

18. Ordinarily, a company's stock price _____ when its reported earnings _____.

19. Freddie Mac steadfastly _____ that its handling of _____ was aimed at _____.

20. Even if it was true that _____ represented the _____ Freddie Mac's _____ had a huge impact that even _____ could not detect _____.

21. Freddie Mac's manipulation did not end there. Another ploy to _____ consisted of ceasing to use _____.

22. Companies can follow a variety of approaches in downplaying expenses such as:

    a. _____

    b. _____

    c. _____

    d. _____

CHAPTER 8: THE APPLICATIONS AND LIMITATIONS OF EBITDA

1. The impetus for trying to redirect investors' focus to _____ or other variants has been _____ recorded by many "new economy" companies.

2. Users of financial statements had discovered certain limitations in net income as a _____. They observed that two companies in the same industry could report similar _____, yet have substantially different _____.

3. Net income is not, to the disappointment of analysts, a standard by which every company's _____ can be compared.

4. The accounting standards leave companies considerable discretion regarding the _____ they assign to their _____. The same applies to amortization schedules for _____.

5. For some companies, the sum of net income, income taxes, and interest expense is not equivalent to EBIT, reflecting the presence of such factors as _____ below _____.

6. Shifting investors' attention away from traditional fixed-charge coverage and toward _____ was particularly beneficial during the 1980s, when some buyouts were so _____ that _____ would not cover pro forma interest expense even in a good year.

7. Capital spending is likely to exceed depreciation over time as the company _____ to accommodate _____. Another reason that capital spending may run higher than depreciation is that newly acquired equipment may be _____ than the old equipment being written off, as a function of _____.

8. Delaying equipment purchases and repairs that are _____ but not _____, should inflict no lasting damage on the company's _____ provided the _____ lasts for only a few quarters.

9. Depreciation is not available as a long-run source of cash for _____. This was a lesson applicable not only to the extremely _____ deals of the 1980s, but also to the more _____ capitalized transactions of later years.

10. Beaver's definition of cash flow was more stringent than _____ since he did not add back either _____ or _____ to net income.

11. Beaver did not conclude that analysts should rely solely on the _____, but merely that it was the single best _____.

12. Some investment managers consider that the single ratio of _____ (as they define it) to _____ predicts bankruptcy better than all of _____ quantitative and qualitative considerations combined.

13. Aside from _____, the amount of working capital needed to run a business represents a fairly constant _____ of a company's sales. Therefore, if inventories or receivables _____ materially as a percentage of sales, analysts should strongly suspect that the earnings are _____, even though management will invariably offer a _____ explanation.

14. If a company resorts to stretching out its payables, two other ratios that will send out warning signals are:
    a. _____
    b. _____

15. Merrill Lynch investment strategist Richard Bernstein points out that _____ earnings tend to be more stable than _____ earnings, EBIT tends to be more stable than _____ earnings, and _____ tends to be more stable than EBIT.

16. Strategist Bernstein found that by attempting to _____ inherent in companies' earnings, investors reduced the _____ of their stock selection.

CHAPTER 9: THE RELIABILITY OF DISCLOSURE AND AUDITS

1. Fear of the consequences of breaking the law keeps corporate managers in line. _____ the law is another matter, though, in the minds of many executives. If their bonuses depend on _____, they can usually see their way clear to adopting that course.

2. Technically, _____ appoints the auditing firm, but _____ is the point of contact in hashing out the details of presenting financial events for _____.

3. At some point, _____ becomes a moral imperative, but in the real world, accounting firms must be _____.

4. It is common for front-line auditors to balk at an _____ proposed by a company's management, only to be overruled by _____.

5. _____ is an unambiguous violation of accounting standards, but audits do not _____.

6. Extremely clever scamsters may even succeed in undermining the auditors' efforts to select _____ a procedure designed to foil concealment of fraud.

7. When challenged on inconsistencies in their numbers, companies sometimes _____, rather than any intention to _____.

8. Seasoned followers of the corporate scene realize that companies are not always as _____ as investors _____.

9. According to president and chief executive of Trump World's Fair Casino Hotel, the firm's focus in 1999 was threefold:
   a. _____
   b. _____
   c. _____

10. Investors who relied solely on _____ by Trump World's Fair Casino Hotel were burned if they bought into the rally that followed the _____ press release.

11. Abundant evidence has emerged over the years of corporate managers _____ to paint as rosy a picture as possible.

12. To say that _____, however, is quite different from saying that
   a. _____
   b. _____
   c. _____ are as good as _____
   d. _____

13. Popular outrage over the _____ accounting scandals created _____ to eliminate _____.

14. Systematic problems in the audit process arise not only _____ but also from _____ of _____.

15. In the 1990s, _____ emerged as a means of keeping a lid on costs. Instead of focusing on _____, they identified the areas that in _____ presented the greatest risk of error or fraud, such as _____. Incredibly, these judgments in some cases were based on _____.

16. In WorldCom's early days, Arthur Andersen audited the company in _____. As the company grew, however, Andersen migrated toward _____. If a question arose about controls or procedures, Andersen relied on the _____.

17. Congress's unwillingness to give the SEC _____ reflected more than _____ on _____.

18. One final line of defense for users of a company's financial statements is _____. This protection has _____ over the years.

19. In one of the few encouraging notes of recent years, the SEC has imposed a _____requirement on audit committee members.

20. Many companies are either _____ or _____. Rather than laying down the law (or GAAP), the auditors typically wind up _____ to arrive at a point where they can convince themselves that _____ have been satisfied.

21. Given the observed gap between _____ and _____ in financial reporting, users of financial statements must provide themselves _____ through tough _____.

CHAPTER 10: MERGERS-AND-ACQUISITIONS ACCOUNTING

1. Choosing a method of accounting for a merger or acquisition does not affect the combined companies' subsequent _____ or _____. The discretionary accounting choices can have a _____, however, on _____.

2. Meyer emphasized that he was _____ Tyco _____, but merely of _____. Nevertheless, the diversified manufacturer responded in the _____; Tyco angrily denounced Meyer's report, stating that _____.

3. Alert analysts had suspected something was going on behind the scenes. They questioned why in the most recent fiscal year, _____ to Tyco's _____ doubled to $21.6 billion even though the company reported $4.8 billion _____.

4. Swartz acknowledged that the amount spent on _____ was not determinable from Tyco's financial statements because it reported _____ and did not disclose the _____.

5. The investigators concluded that Tyco repeatedly used aggressive, _____, including _____ immediately before acquisition, in order to generate _____. Company officials referred

to such practices as _____ and ordered employees to "create stories" to justify _____.

6. Tyco's financial reporting aggressiveness involved _____ through a nonstandard definition of the term. Tyco excluded _____ and _____ for its ADT security-alarm business, labeling the latter _____.

7. Although the pooling-of-interests method has been abolished, M&A accounting remains an area in which analysts must be on their toes. Companies have developed _____ for exploiting the discretion afforded by the rules. _____ in the post-acquisition period remains a key objective.

8. For example, one M&A-related gambit entails the GAAP-sanctioned use, for financial reporting purposes, of _____. Typically, companies use this discretion to simplify the closing of their books at month- or quarter-end.

9. Under Securities and Exchange Commission rules, companies do not have to _____ to reflect the revenues and earnings of acquired businesses _____.

10. There can be no guarantee of loans secured by stock issued in the combination, which would effectively _____ implicit in a bona fide _____. _____ of stock, and are likewise prohibited.

11. Regulators may tighten up rules that can be abused, such as the _____, but corporate managers usually manage to stay one step ahead. Analysts who hope to keep pace would do well to study _____ in order to understand the thought process of the field's most notorious innovators.

12. Clues to hanky-panky may include:
    a. _____
    b. _____, and, if an acquired company was a public reporter prior to its acquisition
    c. _____

CHAPTER 11: IS FRAUD DETECTABLE?

1. Beneish defines manipulation to include both _____ and _____ *within GAAP.*

2. Beneish finds, by statistical analysis, that the presence of any of the following five factors increases the probability of earnings manipulation:

   1. _____
   2. _____
   3. _____
   4. _____
   5. _____

3. The evidence of criminal misrepresentation _____, but _____ definitively identified some of the most famous frauds _____ and the companies _____.

4. In studying these notorious frauds, readers should pay close attention _____, but also _____ as the validity of their stated profits is challenged.

5. Unexpected _____ is a classic warning sign of financial misrepresentation.

6. When Enron at long last conceded that it was overly indebted, management tried to:

   a. _____
   b. _____
   c. _____
   d. _____

7. Enron also misled investors by aggressively exploiting wiggle room in the accounting rules. The company booked revenue from its energy-related derivatives contracts on the basis of _____, rather than _____, as is the norm for _____.

8. Excessive liberties with _____ accounting rules constituted yet one more element of Enron's misrepresentation.

9. On a conference call dealing with Enron's earnings, analyst Richard Grubman complained that the company was _____ in refusing to include a _____ in its earnings release.

10. Still, the _____ vehicles, combined with _____ disclosures, enabled Enron to make itself look less _____ than it really was.

11. While Enron grossly misled investors by _____, a large part of its deception consisted of _____ of basic accounting standards, with _____ of its auditor.

12. Equally crude was a scheme in which Enron reportedly borrowed $500 million from a bank and _____. A few days later it sold _____ and repaid the bank, reporting the proceeds from the meaningless transaction as _____.

13. The _____ of Enron's _____ was a major concern. "Ultimately they're telling you _____, but they're not telling you _____ Business Valuation Services analyst Stephen Campbell complained. "That is essentially saying '_____.'"

14. Off Wall Street Consulting group recommended a short sale of Enron based on two factors identifiable from the financial statements, namely, _____ and _____ with _____.

15. Analysts should be especially wary when _____, as indicated by tools such as _____, coincides with _____ financial reporting.

16. According to the SEC's complaint, HealthSouth's falsification began _____.

17. Flat denial by Scrushy, regardless _____, was a consistent theme as the _____ unfolded.

18. The complaint stated that when HealthSouth officials and accountants urged Scrushy _____, he replied, in effect, "_____."

19. The "Sarbox" provision requiring CFOs and CEOs to attest to the accuracy of financial statements gave prosecutors a powerful weapon to wield against falsifiers, but _____ dispelled any notion that the tough new law _____.

20. HealthSouth exaggerated its earnings by understating the gap between _____ and _____.

21. If the auditors did question an accounting entry, HealthSouth executives reportedly _____ to validate the item.

22. HealthSouth also propped up profits by failing to _____ with _____. In addition, the company _____ when it sold assets _____.

23. Compounding Scushy's legal problems, federal prosecutors disclosed in July 2003 that they had uncovered evidence of:
    a. _____
    b. _____
    c. _____
    d. _____
    e. _____

24. The most dismaying aspect of the performance of HealthSouth's auditor, Ernst & Young LLP, was _____ to challenge a _____ in cash.

25. In the view of experts in the field, internal checks and balances also broke down at HealthSouth. The board's audit committee met _____ during 2001, _____ than the minimum recommended by the SEC.

26. Investors had little official warning of trouble until _____ Parmalat's collapse. As late as October 2003, Deutsche Bank's equity research group rated the company's stock _____, highlighting _____, and Citibank put out _____ report in November. Furthermore, the company's debt carried an _____ rating up until _____ the bankruptcy filing.

27. A major red flag was Parmalat's _____, despite claiming to have a _____.

28. Merrill Lynch analysts downgraded Parmalat to SELL, saying that the company's _____, while reporting _____, threw into question _____.

29. Another hazard signal emerged on February 26, 2003, when Parmalat suddenly canceled its plan _____. The company said it would instead _____, suggesting the market had less confidence in Parmalat's _____ than management had thought.

30. Oddly, the person who achieved the greatest renown for early recognition of the Parmalat's house of cards was _____, but a _____.

CHAPTER 12: FORECASTING
FINANCIAL STATEMENTS

1. It is _____ that determine the value of a company's stock and the _____ that determines credit quality.

2. The process of financial projections is an extension of _____ and _____, based on assumptions about future _____, _____, and _____.

3. Sales projections for the company's business can be developed with the help of such sources as _____, _____, and firms that sell _____ models.

4. Basic industries such as _____, _____, and _____ tend to lend themselves best to the _____ described here. In technology-driven industries and "hits-driven" businesses such as _____ and _____, the connection between _____ and the _____ will tend to be looser.

5. The expected intensity of industry competition, which affects a company's _____ on to customers or to retain _____, influences the _____ forecast.

6. Since the segment information may show only operating income, and not _____, the analyst must add _____ to operating income, then make assumptions about the allocation of _____, _____ and _____ expense by segment.

7. The R&D percentage may change if, for example, the company _____ in an industry that is either significantly more, or significantly less, _____ than its existing operations.

8. The key to the forecasting interest expense method employed here is to estimate the firm's embedded cost of debt, that is, the _____ on the company's _____.

9. Accurately projecting interest expense for _____ companies is important because _____ may depend on the size of _____ they must cover each quarter.

10. The completed income statement projection supplies _____ of the projected statement of cash flows.

11. Before assuming a constant-percentage relationship, the analyst must verify that _____.

12. A sizable _____ might be presumed to be directed toward share repurchase, reducing _____, if management has indicated a desire to _____ and is _____ by its board of directors.

13. Typically, the analyst must modify the underlying _____ assumptions, and therefore the projections, several times during the year as _____ diverges from _____.

14. A firm may have considerable room to cut _____ in the short run if it suffers a decline in funds provided by _____. A projection that ignored this could prove overly pessimistic.

15. An interest rate decline will have limited impact on a company for which interest costs represent a _____. The impact will be greater on a company with a large interest cost component and with much of its debt at _____. This assumes the return on the company's assets is _____.

16. Analysts are generally not arrogant enough to try to forecast the figures accurately to the first decimal place, that is, to the _____ for a company with revenues in the _____.

17. It is generally inappropriate to compare a _____ item (EBITDA) with a balance sheet figure, especially in the case of a _____ company.

18. It is unwise to base an investment decision on historical statements that antedate a major financial change such as:

    a. _____

    b. _____

    c. _____

    d. _____

19. A pro forma income statement for a single year provides no information about _____ in sales and earnings of _____ that is being spun off.

20. Pro forma adjustments for a divestment do not capture the potential benefits of increased _____ on the company's _____.

21. The earnings shown in a merger-related pro forma income statement may be higher than the company can sustain because:

a. The acquired company's owners may be shrewdly selling out at top dollar, anticipating a _____ that is foreseeable by _____, but not to the acquiring corporation's management.

b. Mergers of companies in the same industry often work out poorly due to _____.

c. Inappropriately applying _____ to an industry with very different requirements.

22. A _____ investor buying a 30-year bond is certainly interested in the issuer's financial prospects beyond _____. Similarly, a substantial percentage of the present value of future dividends represented by a stock's price lies _____.

23. Radical financial restructurings such as _____, _____, and _____ necessitate _____ projections.

24. Of the various types of analysis of financial statements, projecting _____ and _____ requires the greatest skill and produces _____.

25. The lack of _____ is what makes financial forecasting so _____. When betting huge sums in the face of _____, it is essential that investors understand _____ as fully as they possibly can.

CHAPTER 13: CREDIT ANALYSIS

1. Financial statements tell much about a borrower's _____ to repay a loan, but disclose little about the equally important _____ to repay.

2. If a company is dependent on raw materials provided by a subsidiary, there may be a _____ presumption that it will stand behind the subsidiary's _____, even _____.

3. Illiquidity manifests itself as an excess of current _____, over _____. The _____ ratio gauges the risk of this occurring by comparing the claims against the company that will become

payable during _____ with the assets that are already in the form of cash or that will be converted to cash during _____.

4. The greater the amount by which asset values could deteriorate, the greater the _____, and the greater the creditor's sense of _____. Equity is by definition _____ minus _____.

5. Aggressive _____ frequently try to satisfy the letter of a _____ leverage limit imposed by lenders, without fulfilling the _____ behind it.

6. A firm that "zeros out" its _____ at some point in each operating cycle can legitimately argue that its "true" leverage is represented by the _____ on its balance sheet.

7. Current maturities of long-term debt should enter into the calculation of _____, based on a conservative assumption that the company will replace maturing debt with _____.

8. Exposure to interest rate fluctuations can also arise from long-term _____. Companies can limit this risk by using _____.

9. Public financial statements typically provide _____ information about the extent to which the issuer has _____ its exposure to interest rate fluctuations through _____.

10. Analysts should remember that the ultimate objective is not to _____ but to _____.

11. In general, the credit analyst must recognize the heightened level of risk implied by the presence of preferred stock in the _____. One formal way to take this risk into account is to calculate the ratio of _____ to _____.

12. In addition to including capital leases in the total debt calculation, analysts should also take into account the _____ liabilities represented by contractual payments on _____, which are reported as _____ in the _____ to Financial Statements.

13. A corporation can employ leverage yet avoid showing debt on its consolidated balance sheet by _____ or forming _____.

14. Under SFAS _____, balance sheet recognition is now given to pension liabilities related to employees' service to date. Similarly, SFAS

_____ requires recognition of postretirement health care benefits as an on-balance sheet liability.

15. The precise formula for _____ a ratio is less important than the assurance that it is _____ for all companies being evaluated.

16. In general, credit analysts should assume that the achievement of _____ bond ratings is a _____ goal of corporate management.

17. The contemporary view is that profits are ultimately what sustain _____ and _____. High profits keep plenty of cash flowing through the system and confirm the value of productive assets such as _____ and _____.

18. The cumulative effect of a change in accounting procedures will appear _____ or after _____ have already been deducted. The sum of net income and provision for income taxes will then differ from the _____ that appears in the income statement.

19. Operating margin shows how well management has run the business _____ wisely, controlling _____ before taking into account financial policies, which largely determine _____, and _____, which is outside management's control.

20. Fixed-charge coverage is an _____ ratio of major interest to credit analysts. It measures the ability of a company's _____ to meet the _____ on its debt, the lender's most direct concern. In its simplest form, the fixed-charge coverage ratio indicates the _____ by which _____ suffice to pay _____.

21. Regardless of whether it is _____ or _____, however, all interest accrued must be covered by _____ and should therefore appear in the _____ of the fixed-charge coverage calculation.

22. The two complications that arise in connection with incorporating operating lease payments into the fixed-charge coverage calculation are:

   a. _____

   b. _____

23. Companies sometimes argue that the denominator of the fixed-charge coverage ratio should include only _____ expense, that

is, the difference between _____ and income derived from _____, generally consisting of marketable securities.

24. Ratios related to sources and uses of funds measure credit quality at the most elemental level—a company's ability to _____.

25. Given corporations' general reluctance to sell new equity, a recurrent cash shortfall is likely to be made up with _____ financing, leading to a rise in _____ ratio.

26. A company that suffers a prolonged downtrend in its ratio of _____ is likely to get more deeply into debt, and therefore become _____ with each succeeding year.

27. Unlike earnings, _____ is essentially a programmed item, a cash flow assured by the accounting rules. The higher the percentage of cash flow derived from _____, the higher is the _____ of a company's cash flow, and the _____ its financial flexibility on the vagaries of the marketplace.

28. Analysts cannot necessarily assume that all is well simply because capital expenditures consistently exceed depreciation. Among the issues to consider are:

   a. _____
   b. _____
   c. _____
   d. _____

29. A limitation of combination ratios that incorporate balance-sheet figures is that they have little meaning if _____.

30. The underlying notion of a turnover ratio is that a company requires a certain level of _____ and _____ to support a given volume of sales.

31. A _____ is a possible explanation of declining inventory turnover. In this case, the inventory may not have suffered a severe reduction in value, but there are nevertheless unfavorable implications for _____. Until the inventory glut can be worked off by _____ to match the lower _____, the company may have to borrow to finance its unusually high working capital, thereby increasing its _____.

32. Fixed-charge coverage, too, has a weakness, for it is based on _____, which are subject to considerable manipulation.

33. Built from two comparatively hard numbers, the ratio of _____ to _____ provides one of the best single measures of _____.

34. Expected _____ have an important bearing on the decision to _____ or _____ credit, as well as on the _____ of debt securities.

35. Line of business is another basis for defining _____.

36. Beyond a certain point, calculating and comparing companies on the basis of _____ financial ratios contributes little _____.

37. _____ or _____ financial ratios can have different implications for different companies.

38. Quantitative models such as Zeta, as well as others that have been devised using various mathematical techniques, have several distinct benefits such as:

    a. _____

    b. _____

    c. _____

39. Like the quantitative models consisting of _____, the default risk models based on stock prices provide useful, but _____, signals.

CHAPTER 14: EQUITY ANALYSIS

1. In this chapter, the discussion focuses primarily on the use of financial statements in _____.

2. Of the methods of fundamental common stock analysis, no other approach matches the intuitive appeal of regarding the stock price as the _____ of expected _____ dividends. This approach is analogous to the _____ calculation for a bond and therefore facilitates the comparison of different _____ of a single _____.

3. By thinking through the logic of the _____ method, the analyst will find that value always comes back to _____.

4. The company's earnings growth rate may diverge from its sales growth due to changes in its _____.

5. As a rule, a _____ company will not increase its dividend on a regular, annual basis.

6. Many analysts argue that _____, rather than _____, is the true determinant of dividend-paying capability.

7. Cash generated from _____, which is generally more difficult for companies to manipulate than _____, can legitimately be viewed as the preferred measure of future _____.

8. The ability to vary the _____, and therefore to assign a _____ or _____ multiple to a company's earnings, is the equity analyst's defense against earnings _____ by management.

9. It is appropriate to assign an _____ discount factor to the earnings of a company that competes against larger, better-capitalized firms. A small company _____ of depth in management and concentration of _____.

10. A building-materials manufacturer may claim to be cushioned against fluctuations in housing starts because of a strong emphasis in its product line on _____.

11. Analysts should be especially wary of companies that have tended to jump on the bandwagon of _____ associated with the _____ of the moment.

12. Earnings per share will not grow merely because _____.

13. Leverage reaches a limit, since lenders will not continue advancing funds beyond a certain point as _____.

14. One way to increase earnings per share is to _____.

15. To the extent that the company funds share buybacks with idle cash, the increase in _____ is offset by a reduction arising from _____.

16. Like most ratio analysis, the Du Pont Formula is valuable not only for _____ but also for _____.

17. Besides introducing greater volatility into the _____, adding debt to the balance sheet demonstrates _____.

18. Some companies have the potential to raise their share prices by _____, while others can increase their value by _____.

19. Management's main adversaries in battles over _____ were aggressive _____.

20. At least in the early stages, before some raiders became overly aggressive in their financial forecast assumptions, it was feasible to extract value without creating undue bankruptcy risk, simply by _____.

21. In future bear markets, when stocks again sell at depressed price-earnings multiples, investors will probably renew their focus on _____.

22. A leveraged buyout can bring about improved profitability for either of two reasons:
    a. _____
    b. _____

23. Today's _____ may be a precursor of tomorrow's bankruptcy by a company that has economized its way to _____.

24. A focus on _____ multiples, the best-known form of fundamental analysis, is not the investor's _____ to relying on technicians' stock charts.

25. For the investor who takes a longer view, _____ provides an invaluable reference point for valuation.

Financial Statement Exercises

1. Indicate in which of the principal financial statements each item appears.
   a.

Item	Balance Sheet	Income Statement	Statement of Cash Flows
Accounts Payable			
Accumulated Depreciation			
Adjusted Net Income			
Capital Expenditures			
Cash and Equivalents—Change			
Common Shares Outstanding			
Current Debt—Changes			
Direct Operating Activities			
Earnings per Share (Fully Diluted)			
Earnings per Share (Primary)			
Equity in Net Loss (Earnings)			
Extraordinary Items			
Financing Activities—Net Cash Flow			
Gross Plant, Property, and Equipment			
Income before Extraordinary Items			
Indirect Operating Activities			
Interest Paid—Net			
Investing Activities			
Investment Tax Credit			
Long-Term Debt Due In One Year			
Minority Interest			
Net Receivables			
Operating Activities—Net Cash Flow			
Other Assets and Liabilities—Net Change			
Other Investments			
Preferred Stock—Nonredeemable			
Pretax Income			
Retained Earnings			
Sale of Property, Plant, and Equipment			
Selling, General, and Administrative Expense			
Stock Equivalents			

Item	Balance Sheet	Income Statement	Statement of Cash Flows
Total Current Assets			
Total Income Taxes			
Total Preferred Stock			

b.

Item	Balance Sheet	Income Statement	Statement of Cash Flows
Accrued Expenses			
Adjusted Available for Common			
Available for Common			
Cash and Equivalents			
Common Equity			
Cost of Goods Sold			
Deferred Taxes			
Dividends per Share			
Earnings per Share (Primary)			
Equity			
Financing Activities			
Funds from Operations—Other			
Income Taxes Paid			
Interest Expense			
Inventory—Decrease (Increase)			
Investing Activities—Other			
Investments at Equity			
Long-Term Debt			
Long-Term Debt—Reduction			
Net Plant, Property, and Equipment			
Notes Payable			
Other Assets			
Other Current Liabilities			
Preferred Dividends			
Prepaid Expenses			
Receivables—Decrease (Increase)			
Sale of Investments			
Savings Due to Common			
Special Items			
Total Assets			
Total Equity			
Total Liabilities and Equity			

c.

Item	Balance Sheet	Income Statement	Statement of Cash Flows
Accounts Payable and Accrued Liabilities—Increase (Decrease)			
Acquisitions			
Assets			
Capital Surplus			
Cash Dividends			
Common Stock			
Deferred Charges			
Discontinued Operations			
Earnings per Share (Fully Diluted)			
EPS from Operations			
Exchange Rate Effect			
Financing Activities—Other			
Gross Profit			
Income Taxes—Accrued—Increase (Decrease)			
Intangibles			
Inventories			
Investing Activities—Net Cash Flow			
Investments—Increase			
Liabilities			
Long-Term Debt—Issuance			
Minority Interest			
Non-Operating Income/Expense			
Operating Profit			
Other Current Assets			
Other Liabilities			
Preferred Stock—Redeemable			
Purchase of Common and Preferred Stock			
Sale of Common and Preferred Stock			
Sales			
Short-Term Investments—Change			
Taxes Payable			
Total Current Liabilities			
Total Liabilities			
Treasury Stock			

2. Construct a common balance sheet from the Balance Sheets of the following firms, determine their operating strategy, and discuss the implications.

Cracker Barrel Old Country Store, Inc. (NasdaqGS:CBRL)
In Millions of USD, except per share items.

	Balance Sheet				
Balance Sheet as of:	Reclassified Jul-28-2006	Aug-03-2007	Aug-01-2008	Jul-31-2009	Jul-30-2010
ASSETS					
Cash and Equivalents	87.8	14.2	12.0	11.6	47.7
Total Cash & ST Investments	**87.8**	**14.2**	**12.0**	**11.6**	**47.7**
Accounts Receivable	11.4	11.8	13.5	12.7	13.5
Other Receivables	0	0	6.9	4.1	0
Total Receivables	**11.4**	**11.8**	**20.4**	**16.8**	**13.5**
Inventory	128.3	144.4	156.0	137.4	144.1
Prepaid Exp.	4.4	12.6	11.0	9.2	8.6
Deferred Tax Assets, Curr.	17.5	12.6	18.1	23.3	22.3
Other Current Assets	404.3	4.7	3.2	0	0
Total Current Assets	**653.8**	**200.3**	**220.6**	**198.3**	**236.3**
Gross Property, Plant & Equipment	1,415.4	1,500.2	1,571.8	1,572.4	1,621.5
Accumulated Depreciation	(432.9)	(481.2)	(526.6)	(570.7)	(617.4)
Net Property, Plant & Equipment	**982.5**	**1,019.0**	**1,045.2**	**1,001.8**	**1,004.1**
Other Long-Term Assets	45.0	45.8	47.8	45.1	51.7
Total Assets	**1,681.3**	**1,265.0**	**1,313.7**	**1,245.2**	**1,292.1**
LIABILITIES					
Accounts Payable	70.9	93.1	93.1	92.2	116.2
Accrued Exp.	139.6	134.2	110.8	110.8	118.4
Curr. Port. of LT Debt	8.1	8.2	8.7	7.4	6.7
Curr. Port. of Cap. Leases	0	0	0	0	0
Curr. Income Taxes Payable	21.4	18.1	0	0	7.6
Unearned Revenue, Current	18.8	21.2	22.6	22.5	27.5
Other Current Liabilities	71.6	0	29.5	32.1	33.0
Total Current Liabilities	**330.5**	**274.7**	**264.7**	**265.0**	**309.5**

	Balance Sheet				
Balance Sheet as of:	Reclassified Jul-28-2006	Aug-03-2007	Aug-01-2008	Jul-31-2009	Jul-30-2010
Long-Term Debt	911.5	756.3	818.7	699.3	640.0
Capital Leases	0	0	0.1	0.1	0
Pension & Other Post-Retire. Benefits	0	0	0	0	25.9
Def. Tax Liability, Non-Curr.	81.9	62.4	54.3	55.7	57.1
Other Non-Current Liabilities	55.1	67.5	83.1	89.6	67.8
Total Liabilities	**1,379.0**	**1,160.9**	**1,221.0**	**1,109.6**	**1,100.5**
Common Stock	0.3	0.2	0.2	0.2	0.2
Additional Paid In Capital	4.3	0	0.7	13.0	6.2
Retained Earnings	302.2	112.9	119.5	167.2	234.0
Treasury Stock	0	0	0	0	0
Comprehensive Inc. and Other	(4.5)	(9.0)	(27.7)	(44.8)	(48.8)
Total Common Equity	**302.3**	**104.1**	**92.8**	**135.6**	**191.6**
Total Equity	**302.3**	**104.1**	**92.8**	**135.6**	**191.6**
Total Liabilities and Equity	**1,681.3**	**1,265.0**	**1,313.7**	**1,245.2**	**1,292.1**
Supplemental Items					
Total Shares Out. on Balance Sheet Date	30.9	23.7	22.3	22.7	22.7
Total Debt	919.6	764.5	827.5	706.8	646.8
Net Debt	831.8	750.2	815.5	695.1	599.1
Debt Equivalent Oper. Leases	434.8	444.1	463.0	483.3	527.0
Finished Goods Inventory	114.3	109.9	142.0	125.2	131.3

(*Continued*)

		Balance Sheet		
Balance Sheet as of:	Reclassified Jul-28-2006	Aug-03-2007	Aug-01-2008	Jul-31-2009	Jul-30-2010
Other Inventory Accounts	14.0	34.5	13.9	12.2	12.8
Land	277.6	287.9	299.6	286.2	287.6
Buildings	967.5	687.0	711.0	686.7	698.4
Machinery	0	336.9	359.1	379.5	410.4
Construction in Progress	17.9	19.7	15.1	16.1	11.5
Leasehold Improvements	149.1	165.5	183.7	200.7	210.3
Full-Time Employees	74,031.0	64,000.0	65,000.0	66,000.0	67,000.0
Assets under Cap. Lease, Gross	3.3	3.3	3.3	3.3	3.3

Chipotle Mexican Grill, Inc. (NYSE:CMG)
In Millions of USD, except per share items.

		Balance Sheet		
Balance Sheet as of:	Dec-31-2005	Dec-31-2006	Dec-31-2007	Dec-31-2008	Dec-31-2009
ASSETS					
Cash and Equivalents	0.1	153.6	151.2	88.0	219.6
Short-Term Investments	0	0	20.0	100.0	50.0
Total Cash & ST Investments	**0.1**	**153.6**	**171.2**	**188.0**	**269.6**
Accounts Receivable	1.9	4.9	5.4	3.6	4.8
Other Receivables	2.2	8.8	9.5	0.3	0
Total Receivables	**4.2**	**13.6**	**14.9**	**3.9**	**4.8**
Inventory	2.6	3.5	4.3	4.8	5.6
Prepaid Exp.	8.6	7.1	9.0	11.8	14.4
Deferred Tax Assets, Curr.	2.3	0.9	2.4	2.6	3.1
Other Current Assets	0	0	0	0	0
Total Current Assets	**17.8**	**178.8**	**201.8**	**211.1**	**297.5**

	Balance Sheet				
Balance Sheet as of:	Dec-31-2005	Dec-31-2006	Dec-31-2007	Dec-31-2008	Dec-31-2009
Gross Property, Plant & Equipment	427.1	522.4	645.9	777.4	882.1
Accumulated Depreciation	(86.4)	(117.6)	(151.0)	(191.5)	(245.7)
Net Property, Plant & Equipment	340.7	404.7	494.9	585.9	636.4
Goodwill	17.7	17.7	21.9	21.9	21.9
Deferred Tax Assets, LT	13.6	0	0	0	0
Other Long-Term Assets	2.7	2.9	3.4	6.1	5.7
Total Assets	392.5	604.2	722.1	825.0	961.5
LIABILITIES					
Accounts Payable	13.2	19.6	19.9	23.9	25.2
Accrued Exp.	23.2	33.1	44.3	44.8	63.3
Curr. Port. of LT Debt	0.1	0.1	0.1	0.1	0.1
Curr. Income Taxes Payable	0	1.5	0	0	4.2
Unearned Revenue, Current	3.7	7.0	9.0	8.0	9.3
Other Current Liabilities	1.8	0	0	0	0
Total Current Liabilities	42.0	61.2	73.3	76.8	102.2
Long-Term Debt	3.5	4.0	4.0	3.9	3.8
Def. Tax Liability, Non-Curr.	0	18.7	16.5	29.9	38.9
Other Non-Current Liabilities	37.7	46.3	66.3	91.9	113.2
Total Liabilities	83.1	130.3	160.0	202.4	258.0
Common Stock	0.3	0.3	0.3	0.3	0.3
Additional Paid In Capital	375.7	470.7	489.3	502.0	539.9
Retained Earnings	(38.5)	3.0	72.5	150.7	277.5
Treasury Stock	0	0	0	(30.2)	(114.3)
Comprehensive Inc. and Other	(28.2)	0	0	(0.2)	0
Total Common Equity	309.4	474.0	562.1	622.6	703.5
Total Equity	309.4	474.0	562.1	622.6	703.5
Total Liabilities and Equity	392.5	604.2	722.1	825.0	961.5

(Continued)

Balance Sheet					
Balance Sheet as of:	Dec-31-2005	Dec-31-2006	Dec-31-2007	Dec-31-2008	Dec-31-2009
Supplemental Items					
Total Shares Out. on Balance Sheet Date	26.3	32.5	32.8	32.2	31.5
Total Debt	3.5	4.1	4.0	4.0	3.9
Net Debt	3.5	(149.5)	(167.1)	(184.1)	(265.7)
Debt Equivalent Oper. Leases	326.9	387.8	560.3	727.6	810.3
Land	6.6	8.2	8.2	8.2	8.9
Buildings	320.9	0	0	0	0
Machinery	99.6	120.2	148.0	179.9	207.0
Leasehold Improvements	320.9	394.0	489.8	589.3	666.2
Full-Time Employees	13,000.0	15,000.0	18,800.0	20,400.0	22,250.0

Buffalo Wild Wings Inc. (NasdaqGS:BWLD)
In Millions of USD, except per share items.

Balance Sheet					
Balance Sheet as of:	Dec-25-2005	Dec-31-2006	Dec-30-2007	Reclassified Dec-28-2008	Dec-27-2009
ASSETS					
Cash and Equivalents	4.0	11.8	1.5	8.3	9.6
Short-Term Investments	48.4	52.8	66.5	36.2	43.6
Total Cash & ST Investments	**52.4**	**64.6**	**68.0**	**44.5**	**53.2**
Accounts Receivable	0.7	0.9	0.9	0.9	2.1
Other Receivables	3.7	5.2	8.9	7.4	9.3
Total Receivables	**4.4**	**6.1**	**9.7**	**8.3**	**11.4**
Inventory	1.5	1.8	2.4	3.1	3.6
Prepaid Exp.	2.0	1.1	3.1	3.3	3.0
Deferred Tax Assets, Curr.	0.8	1.4	1.3	1.7	2.9
Other Current Assets	0	0	—	7.7	24.4
Total Current Assets	**61.1**	**75.0**	**84.5**	**68.6**	**98.5**
Gross Property, Plant & Equipment	110.8	132.8	169.7	235.6	298.1
Accumulated Depreciation	(42.1)	(54.7)	(67.0)	(81.2)	(108.4)
Net Property, Plant & Equipment	**68.7**	**78.1**	**102.7**	**154.4**	**189.6**

			Balance Sheet		
Balance Sheet as of:	Dec-25-2005	Dec-31-2006	Dec-30-2007	Reclassified Dec-28-2008	Dec-27-2009
Goodwill	0.4	0.4	0.4	11.0	11.2
Other Intangibles	0.3	0.4	0.4	7.3	6.7
Other Long-Term Assets	2.7	7.4	9.1	2.5	3.0
Total Assets	**133.1**	**161.2**	**197.1**	**243.8**	**309.1**
LIABILITIES					
Accounts Payable	6.6	5.9	10.7	16.7	13.4
Accrued Exp.	10.7	16.5	18.8	18.6	26.1
Curr. Income Taxes Payable	0.1	0.3	—	0	0
Unearned Revenue, Current	2.2	2.3	2.3	2.5	2.7
Other Current Liabilities	0.6	0.8	0.7	10.4	24.5
Total Current Liabilities	**20.2**	**25.8**	**32.5**	**48.2**	**66.7**
Def. Tax Liability, Non-Curr.	4.8	3.2	2.2	8.9	14.9
Other Non-Current Liabilities	11.3	16.0	20.8	15.1	17.6
Total Liabilities	**36.3**	**45.0**	**55.4**	**72.2**	**99.2**
Common Stock	74.5	75.0	80.8	86.3	93.9
Additional Paid In Capital	0	0	—	0	0
Retained Earnings	24.9	41.2	60.8	85.3	115.9
Treasury Stock	0	0	—	0	0
Comprehensive Inc. and Other	(2.6)	0	—	0	0
Total Common Equity	**96.8**	**116.2**	**141.7**	**171.6**	**209.8**
Total Equity	**96.8**	**116.2**	**141.7**	**171.6**	**209.8**
Total Liabilities and Equity	**133.1**	**161.2**	**197.1**	**243.8**	**309.1**
Supplemental Items					
Total Shares Out. on Balance Sheet Date	17.2	17.6	17.7	17.9	18.1
Net Debt	(52.4)	(64.6)	(68.0)	(44.5)	(53.2)
Debt Equivalent Oper. Leases	96.7	120.9	138.7	179.0	223.2
Buildings	64.5	NA	1.6	6.6	18.3
Machinery	45.3	54.0	70.0	95.5	121.2
Construction in Progress	1.0	1.0	1.9	10.7	6.4
Leasehold Improvements	64.5	77.8	96.3	122.8	152.1
Full-Time Employees	1,282.0	1,113.0	988.0	1,200.0	1,200.0
Part-Time Employees	4,843.0	6,210.0	8,576.0	10,800.0	12,800.0

Denny's Corporation (NasdaqCM:DENN)
In Millions of USD, except per share items.

			Balance Sheet		
Balance Sheet as of:	Restated Dec-28-2005	Restated Dec-27-2006	Restated Dec-26-2007	Restated Dec-31-2008	Dec-30-2009
ASSETS					
Cash and Equivalents	28.2	26.2	21.6	21.0	26.5
Total Cash & ST Investments	28.2	26.2	21.6	21.0	26.5
Accounts Receivable	16.8	15.0	13.6	15.1	18.1
Notes Receivable	0	0	0	0	0
Total Receivables	16.8	15.0	13.6	15.1	18.1
Inventory	8.2	8.2	6.5	5.5	4.2
Prepaid Exp.	8.4	9.1	9.5	9.5	9.5
Other Current Assets	0	4.7	6.7	2.3	0
Total Current Assets	61.6	63.2	57.9	53.5	58.3
Gross Property, Plant & Equipment	669.9	615.5	491.7	444.9	390.2
Accumulated Depreciation	(381.7)	(379.3)	(307.0)	(284.9)	(258.7)
Net Property, Plant & Equipment	288.1	236.3	184.6	160.0	131.5
Goodwill	50.2	50.1	42.4	34.6	32.4
Other Intangibles	71.7	73.6	69.0	64.4	59.5
Loans Receivable Long-Term	0	0	0	0	0
Deferred Charges, LT	15.8	6.3	5.1	3.9	2.7
Other Long-Term Assets	23.9	14.9	18.4	25.5	28.2
Total Assets	511.3	444.4	377.4	341.8	312.6
LIABILITIES					
Accounts Payable	47.6	42.1	43.3	25.3	22.8
Accrued Exp.	70.6	52.5	58.8	52.4	43.9
Curr. Port. of LT Debt	1.9	5.5	2.1	1.4	0.9
Curr. Port. of Cap. Leases	6.2	7.0	4.1	3.5	3.7
Curr. Income Taxes Payable	0	11.8	9.7	8.8	8.0
Other Current Liabilities	22.1	16.9	13.6	15.7	12.8
Total Current Liabilities	148.4	135.8	131.5	107.1	92.1

	Balance Sheet				
Balance Sheet as of:	Restated Dec-28-2005	Restated Dec-27-2006	Restated Dec-26-2007	Restated Dec-31-2008	Dec-30-2009
Long-Term Debt	516.8	415.8	326.0	300.6	258.9
Capital Leases	28.9	24.9	20.8	22.1	19.7
Pension & Other Post-Retire. Benefits	0	0	3.7	15.2	9.9
Def. Tax Liability, Non-Curr.	0	12.1	11.6	12.3	13.0
Other Non-Current Liabilities	83.7	79.3	66.1	63.9	46.5
Total Liabilities	777.8	667.9	559.6	521.2	440.1
Common Stock	0.9	0.9	0.9	1.0	1.0
Additional Paid In Capital	517.9	527.9	533.6	538.9	542.6
Retained Earnings	(765.8)	(735.0)	(703.6)	(694.4)	(652.8)
Treasury Stock	0	0	0	0	0
Comprehensive Inc. and Other	(19.5)	(17.4)	(13.1)	(24.9)	(18.2)
Total Common Equity	(266.5)	(223.6)	(182.2)	(179.4)	(127.5)
Total Equity	(266.5)	(223.6)	(182.2)	(179.4)	(127.5)
Total Liabilities and Equity	511.3	444.4	377.4	341.8	312.6
Supplemental Items					
Total Shares Out. on Balance Sheet Date	91.8	93.2	94.6	95.7	96.6
Total Debt	553.8	453.3	353.0	327.6	283.2
Net Debt	525.5	427.0	331.4	306.6	256.7
Debt Equiv. of Unfunded Proj. Benefit Obligation	15.9	9.9	0.8	12.8	7.7
Debt Equivalent Oper. Leases	409.8	405.3	400.1	398.3	390.4
Finished Goods Inventory	0	0	6.5	5.5	4.2

(Continued)

	Balance Sheet				
Balance Sheet as of:	Restated Dec-28- 2005	Restated Dec-27- 2006	Restated Dec-26- 2007	Restated Dec-31- 2008	Dec-30- 2009
Land	56.9	37.5	28.8	23.7	18.0
Buildings	474.9	393.2	279.4	243.2	209.0
Machinery	138.1	0	0	0	0
Full-Time Employees	27,000.0	27,000.0	21,000.0	15,000.0	11,000.0
Assets under Cap. Lease, Gross	37.6	39.6	20.6	19.3	12.3
Assets under Cap. Lease, Accum. Depr.	(17.0)	(20.2)	(12.2)	(10.5)	(5.9)
Assets on Oper. Lease, Gross	0	0	48.1	56.5	61.0
Assets on Oper. Lease, Accum. Depr.	0	0	(35.1)	(37.0)	(40.0)

California Pizza Kitchen Inc. (NasdaqGS:CPKI)
In Millions of USD, except per share items.

	Balance Sheet				
Balance Sheet as of:	Jan-01- 2006	Reclassified Dec-31- 2006	Reclassified Dec-30- 2007	Dec-28- 2008	Jan-03- 2010
ASSETS					
Cash and Equivalents	11.3	8.2	10.8	14.4	21.4
Short-Term Investments	11.4	0	0	0	0
Total Cash & ST Investments	**22.7**	**8.2**	**10.8**	**14.4**	**21.4**
Accounts Receivable	4.1	7.9	2.0	2.8	3.2
Other Receivables	0	0	10.3	7.1	9.3
Total Receivables	**4.1**	**7.9**	**12.4**	**9.9**	**12.5**
Inventory	3.8	4.7	5.2	5.4	5.6
Prepaid Exp.	5.5	5.4	5.8	1.9	7.0
Deferred Tax Assets, Curr.	8.4	11.7	7.0	6.0	7.1
Other Current Assets	1.4	0	0	0	0
Total Current Assets	**45.9**	**37.9**	**41.2**	**37.5**	**53.6**

	Balance Sheet				
Balance Sheet as of:	Jan-01-2006	Reclassified Dec-31-2006	Reclassified Dec-30-2007	Dec-28-2008	Jan-03-2010
Gross Property, Plant & Equipment	399.3	467.9	543.5	591.0	602.9
Accumulated Depreciation	(185.9)	(212.5)	(245.7)	(295.5)	(347.5)
Net Property, Plant & Equipment	213.4	255.4	297.9	295.5	255.4
Goodwill	0	0	0	4.6	4.6
Other Intangibles	6.0	7.8	8.8	4.9	4.7
Deferred Tax Assets, LT	4.5	5.9	13.8	20.7	25.0
Other Long-Term Assets	4.4	3.6	5.5	5.2	6.9
Total Assets	274.3	310.5	367.1	368.4	350.3
LIABILITIES					
Accounts Payable	7.1	15.0	20.0	12.3	11.3
Accrued Exp.	35.6	42.8	49.7	49.5	53.4
Curr. Port. of LT Debt	0	0	21.0	0	0
Curr. Income Taxes Payable	0	3.6	1.0	4.1	0
Unearned Revenue, Current	0	0	8.0	9.7	20.6
Other Current Liabilities	4.1	4.5	9.2	3.8	4.1
Total Current Liabilities	46.7	66.0	108.9	79.5	89.4
Long-Term Debt	0	0	0	74.0	22.3
Pension & Other Post-Retire. Benefits	0	0	0	1.2	1.6
Other Non-Current Liabilities	30.2	36.1	40.1	39.2	47.7
Total Liabilities	76.9	102.2	149.0	193.9	161.0
Common Stock	0.2	0.3	0.3	0.2	0.2
Additional Paid In Capital	231.2	221.1	216.0	163.8	174.0
Retained Earnings	(34.0)	(13.0)	1.8	10.5	15.0
Treasury Stock	0	0	0	0	0
Comprehensive Inc. and Other	0	0	0	0	0
Total Common Equity	197.3	208.3	218.1	174.5	189.3

(*Continued*)

		Balance Sheet			
Balance Sheet as of:	Jan-01-2006	Reclassified Dec-31-2006	Reclassified Dec-30-2007	Dec-28-2008	Jan-03-2010
Total Equity	197.3	208.3	218.1	174.5	189.3
Total Liabilities and Equity	274.3	310.5	367.1	368.4	350.3
Supplemental Items					
Total Shares Out. on Balance Sheet Date	29.5	28.9	28.4	23.9	24.2
Total Debt	0	0	21.0	74.0	22.3
Net Debt	(22.7)	(8.2)	10.2	59.6	0.9
Debt Equivalent Oper. Leases	182.8	219.2	252.8	304.0	304.8
Land	5.8	5.8	5.8	5.8	5.8
Buildings	237.5	10.1	10.1	10.6	11.3
Machinery	139.5	151.9	174.7	196.8	192.4
Construction in Progress	16.5	40.5	37.4	35.6	6.4
Leasehold Improvements	227.4	259.7	315.6	342.3	387.1
Full-Time Employees	12,900.0	13,900.0	14,800.0	15,100.0	14,600.0

3. Construct a common size income statement from the Income Statement of the following firms, determine their operating strategy, and discuss the implications.

Cracker Barrel Old Country Store, Inc. (NasdaqGS:CBRL)
In Millions of USD, except per share items.

		Income Statement			
For the Fiscal Period Ending	Reclassified Jul-28-2006	Reclassified Aug-03-2007	Aug-01-2008	Jul-31-2009	Jul-30-2010
Total Revenue	2,219.5	2,351.6	2,384.5	2,367.3	2,404.5
Cost of Goods Sold	1,539.0	1,637.1	1,683.3	1,681.2	1,654.0
Gross Profit	680.4	714.5	701.2	686.1	750.5
Selling General & Admin Exp.	512.1	547.6	549.6	541.8	583.0

	Income Statement				
For the Fiscal Period Ending	Reclassified Jul-28- 2006	Reclassified Aug-03- 2007	Aug-01- 2008	Jul-31- 2009	Jul-30- 2010
R & D Exp.	0	0	0	0	0
Depreciation & Amort.	0	0	0	0	0
Other Operating Expense/(Income)	0	0	0	0	0
Other Operating Exp., Total	512.1	547.6	549.6	541.8	583.0
Operating Income	168.4	166.8	151.7	144.3	167.5
Interest Expense	(22.2)	(59.4)	(57.4)	(52.2)	(49.0)
Interest and Invest. Income	0.8	7.8	0.2	0	0
Net Interest Exp.	(21.4)	(51.7)	(57.3)	(52.2)	(49.0)
Other Non-Operating Inc. (Exp.)	0	0	0	0	0
EBT Excl. Unusual Items	146.9	115.2	94.4	92.2	118.5
Restructuring Charges	(6.6)	0	0	0	0
Impairment of Goodwill	0	0	0	0	0
Asset Writedown	0	0	(0.9)	(2.1)	(2.8)
Legal Settlements	0	1.3	0	0	0
Other Unusual Items	0	0	0	0	0
EBT Incl. Unusual Items	140.4	116.5	93.5	90.1	115.7
Income Tax Expense	44.9	40.5	28.2	24.1	30.5
Earnings from Cont. Ops.	95.5	76.0	65.3	66.0	85.3
Earnings of Discontinued Ops.	20.8	86.1	0.3	0	0
Extraord. Item & Account. Change	0	0	0	0	0
Net Income	116.3	162.1	65.6	65.9	85.3
Dividends per Share	$0.52	$0.56	$0.72	$0.8	$0.8
Payout Ratio %	20.7%	9.6%	24.0%	26.7%	21.8%

(*Continued*)

Income Statement

For the Fiscal Period Ending	Reclassified Jul-28-2006	Reclassified Aug-03-2007	Aug-01-2008	Jul-31-2009	Jul-30-2010
Supplemental Items					
EBITDA	225.6	223.7	209.3	203.6	228.5
EBITA	168.4	166.8	151.7	144.3	167.5
EBIT	168.4	166.8	151.7	144.3	167.5
EBITDAR	280.0	279.2	267.2	264.0	294.4
Supplemental Operating Expense Items					
Advertising Exp.	38.3	40.5	42.2	42.4	45.2
General and Administrative Exp.	128.8	136.2	127.3	120.2	145.9
Net Rental Exp.	54.3	55.5	57.9	60.4	65.9
Imputed Oper. Lease Interest Exp.	17.4	31.8	33.8	33.2	38.3
Imputed Oper. Lease Depreciation	37.0	23.7	24.1	27.3	27.6

Chipotle Mexican Grill, Inc. (NYSE:CMG)
In Millions of USD, except per share items.

Income Statement

For the Fiscal Period Ending	Dec-31-2005	Dec-31-2006	Reclassified Dec-31-2007	Reclassified Dec-31-2008	Dec-31-2009
Total Revenue	627.7	822.9	1,085.8	1,332.0	1,518.4
Cost of Goods Sold	428.6	547.9	711.7	878.4	965.3
Gross Profit	199.1	275.0	374.1	453.5	553.1
Selling General & Admin Exp.	52.0	68.0	98.3	117.1	124.5
Pre-Opening Costs	2.0	4.1	5.0	5.7	4.0
R & D Exp.	0	0	0	0	0
Depreciation & Amort.	28.0	34.3	43.6	52.8	61.3
Other Operating Expense/(Income)	83.0	102.7	112.9	142.0	153.6
Other Operating Exp., Total	164.9	209.1	259.7	317.6	343.4

		Income Statement			
For the Fiscal Period Ending	Dec-31-2005	Dec-31-2006	Reclassified Dec-31-2007	Reclassified Dec-31-2008	Dec-31-2009
Operating Income	34.1	65.9	114.4	136.0	209.7
Interest Expense	(0.8)	(0.3)	(0.3)	(0.3)	(0.4)
Interest and Invest. Income	0	6.6	6.1	3.5	0.9
Net Interest Exp.	(0.8)	6.3	5.8	3.2	0.5
Other Non-Operating Inc. (Exp.)	0	0	0	0	0
EBT Excl. Unusual Items	33.4	72.2	120.2	139.1	210.2
Impairment of Goodwill	0	0	0	0	0
Gain (Loss) on Sale of Assets	(3.1)	(4.0)	(6.2)	(9.3)	(6.0)
Other Unusual Items	0	0	0	(2.6)	0
EBT Incl. Unusual Items	30.2	68.3	114.0	127.2	204.2
Income Tax Expense	(7.5)	26.8	43.4	49.0	77.4
Earnings from Cont. Ops.	37.7	41.4	70.6	78.2	126.8
Earnings of Discontinued Ops.	0	0	0	0	0
Extraord. Item & Account. Change	0	0	0	0	0
Net Income	37.7	41.4	70.6	78.2	126.8
Supplemental Items					
EBITDA	62.1	100.2	157.9	188.7	271.0
EBITA	34.1	65.9	114.4	136.0	209.7
EBIT	34.1	65.9	114.4	136.0	209.7
EBITDAR	103.0	148.7	228.0	279.7	372.3
Supplemental Operating Expense Items					
Advertising Exp.	10.7	13.9	0	0	0
Marketing Exp.	0	0	18.6	22.1	21.0
Selling and Marketing Exp.	0	0	18.6	22.1	21.0

(Continued)

Income Statement

For the Fiscal Period Ending	Dec-31-2005	Dec-31-2006	Reclassified Dec-31-2007	Reclassified Dec-31-2008	Dec-31-2009
General and Administrative Exp.	52.0	65.3	75.0	89.2	99.1
Net Rental Exp.	40.9	48.5	70.0	90.9	101.3
Imputed Oper. Lease Interest Exp.	64.9	27.5	40.7	55.0	83.7
Imputed Oper. Lease Depreciation	(24.0)	21.0	29.3	36.0	17.6

Buffalo Wild Wings Inc. (NasdaqGS:BWLD)
In Millions of USD, except per share items.

Income Statement

For the Fiscal Period Ending	Reclassified Dec-25-2005	Reclassified Dec-31-2006	Dec-30-2007	Dec-28-2008	Dec-27-2009
Total Revenue	209.7	278.2	329.7	422.4	538.9
Cost of Goods Sold	158.1	207.7	245.8	313.2	402.9
	51.6	70.5	83.8	109.2	136.0
Selling General & Admin Exp.	22.3	30.4	35.7	40.2	49.4
Pre-Opening Costs	2.6	3.1	4.5	7.9	7.7
R & D Exp.	—	0	0	0	0
Depreciation & Amort.	11.8	14.5	17.0	23.6	32.6
Other Operating Expense/(Income)	0	0	0	0	0
Other Operating Exp., Total	36.7	47.9	57.2	71.7	89.7
Operating Income	15.0	22.5	26.6	37.5	46.3
Interest Expense	0	0	0	0	0
Interest and Invest. Income	1.3	2.3	2.9	1.0	1.1
Net Interest Exp.	1.3	2.3	2.9	1.0	1.1

	Income Statement				
For the Fiscal Period Ending	Reclassified Dec-25-2005	Reclassified Dec-31-2006	Dec-30-2007	Dec-28-2008	Dec-27-2009
Other Non-Operating Inc. (Exp.)	0	0	0	0	0
EBT Excl. Unusual Items	**16.3**	**24.8**	**29.5**	**38.4**	**47.4**
Restructuring Charges	(2.0)	(1.0)	0	0	0
Impairment of Goodwill	0	0	0	0	0
Asset Writedown	0	0	(1.0)	(2.1)	(1.9)
Other Unusual Items	0	0	0	0	0
EBT Incl. Unusual Items	**14.3**	**23.8**	**28.5**	**36.4**	**45.4**
Income Tax Expense	5.4	7.6	8.9	11.9	14.8
Earnings from Cont. Ops.	**8.9**	**16.3**	**19.7**	**24.4**	**30.7**
Earnings of Discontinued Ops.	0	0	0	0	0
Extraord. Item & Account. Change	0	0	0	0	0
Net Income	**8.9**	**16.3**	**19.7**	**24.4**	**30.7**
Supplemental Items					
EBITDA	26.8	36.9	43.5	61.1	78.9
EBITA	15.1	22.5	26.5	37.7	46.9
EBIT	15.0	22.5	26.6	37.5	46.3
EBITDAR	38.9	52.1	60.9	83.5	106.8
Supplemental Operating Expense Items					
Advertising Exp.	5.8	9.1	10.5	13.5	17.8
General and Administrative Exp.	22.3	30.4	35.7	40.2	49.4
Net Rental Exp.	12.1	15.1	17.3	22.4	27.9

California Pizza Kitchen Inc. (NasdaqGS:CPKI)
In Millions of USD, except per share items.

	Income Statement				
For the Fiscal Period Ending	Jan-01-2006	Dec-31-2006	Dec-30-2007	Dec-28-2008	Jan-03-2010
Total Revenue	479.6	554.6	632.9	677.1	664.7
Cost of Goods Sold	385.1	444.2	507.1	553.2	543.5
Gross Profit	94.5	110.5	125.8	123.9	121.2
Selling General & Admin Exp.	36.3	43.3	48.4	52.4	52.4
Pre-Opening Costs	4.1	7.0	7.2	4.5	1.8
R & D Exp.	0	0	0	0	0
Depreciation & Amort.	25.4	29.5	37.1	40.3	40.2
Other Operating Expense/(Income)	0	0	0	0	0
Other Operating Exp., Total	65.8	79.8	92.7	97.2	94.4
Operating Income	28.8	30.7	33.1	26.8	26.8
Interest Expense	0	0	(0.1)	(1.3)	(0.8)
Interest and Invest. Income	0.7	0.7	0	0	0
Net Interest Exp.	0.7	0.7	(0.1)	(1.3)	(0.8)
Income/(Loss) from Affiliates	0	0	0	0	0
Other Non-Operating Inc. (Exp.)	0	0	0	0	0
EBT Excl. Unusual Items	29.5	31.4	33.0	25.4	26.0
Restructuring Charges	(0.2)	(0.7)	(9.3)	(1.0)	(0.5)
Impairment of Goodwill	0	0	0	0	0
Asset Writedown	(1.2)	0	0	(13.3)	(22.9)
Legal Settlements	(0.6)	0	(2.3)	0	0
Other Unusual Items	1.1	0	0	0	0
EBT Incl. Unusual Items	28.7	30.7	21.4	11.1	2.5
Income Tax Expense	9.2	9.7	6.7	2.4	(2.1)
Earnings from Cont. Ops.	19.5	21.0	14.8	8.7	4.6

Income Statement

For the Fiscal Period Ending	Jan-01-2006	Dec-31-2006	Dec-30-2007	Dec-28-2008	Jan-03-2010
Earnings of Discontinued Ops.	0	0	0	0	0
Extraord. Item & Account. Change	0	0	0	0	0
Net Income	<u>19.5</u>	<u>21.0</u>	<u>14.8</u>	<u>8.7</u>	<u>4.6</u>
Supplemental Items					
EBITDA	54.2	60.2	70.2	67.0	66.9
EBITA	28.8	30.7	33.1	26.9	26.9
EBIT	28.8	30.7	33.1	26.8	26.8
EBITDAR	77.0	87.6	101.8	105.0	105.0
Supplemental Operating Expense Items					
Advertising Exp.	4.2	4.9	5.5	6.6	7.4
General and Administrative Exp.	36.3	43.3	48.4	52.4	52.4
Net Rental Exp.	22.8	27.4	31.6	38.0	38.1
Imputed Oper. Lease Interest Exp.	0	0	0	14.0	5.4
Imputed Oper. Lease Depreciation	0	0	0	24.0	32.7

Denny's Corporation (NasdaqCM:DENN)
In Millions of USD, except per share items.

Income Statement

For the Fiscal Period Ending	Reclassified Dec-28-2005	Reclassified Dec-27-2006	Restated Dec-26-2007	Restated Dec-31-2008	Dec-30-2009
Total Revenue	978.7	994.0	939.4	760.3	608.1
Cost of Goods Sold	695.9	696.5	668.9	519.4	396.9
Gross Profit	282.8	297.5	270.4	240.9	211.2
Selling General & Admin Exp.	91.3	96.3	94.8	84.2	77.4
R & D Exp.	0	0	0	0	0

(Continued)

Income Statement					
For the Fiscal Period Ending	Reclassified Dec-28-2005	Reclassified Dec-27-2006	Restated Dec-26-2007	Restated Dec-31-2008	Dec-30-2009
Depreciation & Amort.	56.1	55.3	49.3	39.8	32.3
Other Operating Expense/(Income)	75.5	81.6	73.9	60.1	43.1
Other Operating Exp., Total	223.0	233.2	218.1	184.0	152.8
Operating Income	59.8	64.3	52.3	56.8	58.4
Interest Expense	(56.8)	(59.5)	(44.3)	(36.7)	(34.3)
Interest and Invest. Income	1.6	1.8	1.4	1.3	1.7
Net Interest Exp.	(55.2)	(57.7)	(43.0)	(35.5)	(32.6)
Other Non-Operating Inc. (Exp.)	0.4	(0.9)	(0.6)	(7.5)	2.2
EBT Excl. Unusual Items	5.1	5.7	8.7	13.9	28.0
Restructuring Charges	(5.2)	(6.2)	(6.9)	(9.0)	(4.0)
Impairment of Goodwill	0	0	0	0	0
Gain (Loss) on Sale of Invest.	0.2	0.5	0.5	(1.7)	1.0
Gain (Loss) on Sale of Assets	3.3	56.8	39.0	18.7	19.4
Asset Writedown	(1.2)	(2.7)	(1.1)	(3.3)	(1.0)
Legal Settlements	(8.3)	(1.7)	(3.6)	(2.3)	(0.4)
Other Unusual Items	0	(7.6)	(0.5)	0	(0.1)
EBT Incl. Unusual Items	(6.1)	44.8	36.2	16.3	43.0
Income Tax Expense	1.2	14.7	6.7	3.5	1.4
Earnings from Cont. Ops.	(7.3)	30.1	29.5	12.7	41.6
Earnings of Discontinued Ops.	0	0	0	0	0
Extraord. Item & Account. Change	0	0.2	0	0	0
Net Income	(7.3)	30.3	29.5	12.7	41.6

	Income Statement				
For the Fiscal Period Ending	Reclassified Dec-28- 2005	Reclassified Dec-27- 2006	Restated Dec-26- 2007	Restated Dec-31- 2008	Dec-30- 2009
Supplemental Operating Expense Items					
Marketing Exp.	28.4	29.9	27.5	23.2	20.1
Selling and Marketing Exp.	28.4	29.9	27.5	23.2	20.1
General and Administrative Exp.	62.9	66.4	67.4	61.0	57.3
Net Rental Exp.	51.2	50.7	50.0	49.8	48.8
Imputed Oper. Lease Interest Exp.	42.1	47.9	44.0	43.0	43.9
Imputed Oper. Lease Depreciation	9.2	2.7	6.0	6.8	4.9
Maintenance & Repair Exp.	18.7	18.3	18.3	14.6	9.9

4. For the firms listed below, determine the stage of growth based an analysis of their financial statements.

L-1 Identity Solutions Inc. (NYSE:ID)
In Millions USD, except per share items.

	Balance Sheet				
Balance Sheet as of:	Dec-31- 2005	Dec-31- 2006	Restated Dec-31- 2007	Restated Dec-31- 2008	Dec-31- 2009
ASSETS					
Cash and Equivalents	72.4	5.0	8.2	20.4	6.6
Total Cash & ST Investments	72.4	5.0	8.2	20.4	6.6
Accounts Receivable	14.6	61.5	90.2	105.6	116.4
Total Receivables	14.6	61.5	90.2	105.6	116.4
Inventory	4.9	11.0	21.5	34.5	29.4
Deferred Tax Assets, Curr.	—	—	13.3	11.1	11.5
Other Current Assets	0.9	4.5	3.9	9.6	9.2
Total Current Assets	92.9	82.0	137.1	181.3	173.1

(Continued)

	Balance Sheet				
Balance Sheet as of:	Dec-31-2005	Dec-31-2006	Restated Dec-31-2007	Restated Dec-31-2008	Dec-31-2009
Gross Property, Plant & Equipment	60.6	58.5	69.5	133.5	190.3
Accumulated Depreciation	(41.1)	(38.6)	(46.0)	(52.3)	(74.8)
Net Property, Plant & Equipment	**19.5**	**19.9**	**23.5**	**81.3**	**115.5**
Goodwill	152.2	951.4	1,054.3	891.0	889.8
Other Intangibles	27.3	170.1	184.2	108.3	102.4
Deferred Tax Assets, LT	—	—	37.3	23.6	26.7
Other Long-Term Assets	2.3	3.8	9.3	24.4	16.3
Total Assets	**294.1**	**1,227.2**	**1,445.6**	**1,309.8**	**1,323.8**
LIABILITIES					
Accounts Payable	9.4	24.5	48.5	72.5	73.4
Accrued Exp.	2.0	30.3	33.1	45.6	36.7
Curr. Port. of LT Debt	—	—	—	19.3	27.1
Unearned Revenue, Current	2.6	10.3	12.3	17.0	19.9
Other Current Liabilities	1.4	5.2	2.4	2.6	6.7
Total Current Liabilities	**15.4**	**70.3**	**96.2**	**156.9**	**163.7**
Long-Term Debt	—	80.0	259.0	429.2	419.3
Minority Interest	—	—	—	—	0.3
Unearned Revenue, Non-Current	1.7	3.7	4.7	13.3	6.7
Def. Tax Liability, Non-Curr.	2.0	4.4	—	—	—
Other Non-Current Liabilities	0.4	1.7	1.0	1.9	3.7
Total Liabilities	**19.4**	**160.1**	**360.9**	**601.3**	**593.6**
Pref. Stock, Convertible	—	—	—	15.1	—
Total Pref. Equity	**—**	**—**	**—**	**15.1**	**—**
Common Stock	0	0.1	0.1	0.1	0.1
Additional Paid in Capital	333.5	1,153.8	1,217.8	1,393.8	1,432.9
Retained Earnings	(56.4)	(87.5)	(69.8)	(623.3)	(627.4)

		Balance Sheet			
Balance Sheet as of:	Dec-31-2005	Dec-31-2006	Restated Dec-31-2007	Restated Dec-31-2008	Dec-31-2009
Treasury Stock	—	—	—	(6.2)	(6.2)
Comprehensive Inc. and Other	(2.4)	0.7	(63.4)	(71.1)	(69.2)
Total Common Equity	274.7	1,067.1	1,084.7	693.4	730.2
Total Equity	274.7	1,067.1	1,084.7	708.5	730.2
Total Liabilities and Equity	294.1	1,227.2	1,445.6	1,309.8	1,323.8
Supplemental Items Total Shares Out. on Filing Date	29.0	72.6	75.2	86.5	92.3

L-1 Identity Solutions Inc. (NYSE:ID)
In Millions of USD, except per share items.

		Analysis (selected items)			
For the Fiscal Period Ending	Dec-31-2005	Dec-31-2006	Dec-31-2007	Dec-31-2008	Dec-31-2009
Total Revenue	66.2	164.4	389.5	562.9	650.9
Gross Profit	23.7	64.7	148.2	192.7	200.1
Selling General & Admin Exp.	19.9	44.4	90.0	123.8	133.9
Net Income	(7.4)	(31.0)	15.8	(551.6)	(4.2)
Cash from Ops.	4.4	12.6	41.0	52.8	60.6
Cash from Investing	(42.9)	(162.4)	(151.9)	(350.9)	(66.2)
Cash from Financing	99.6	82.3	114.1	310.8	(8.5)
Total Debt Issued	0.2	80.0	179.0	295.0	24.9
Total Debt Repaid	(0.3)	(0.3)	(0.8)	(88.8)	(35.1)
Net Interest Exp.	0.2	0.2	(10.9)	(23.1)	(32.7)

(*Continued*)

Analysis (selected items)					
For the Fiscal Period Ending	Dec-31-2005	Dec-31-2006	Dec-31-2007	Dec-31-2008	Dec-31-2009
Issuance of Common Stock	99.6	7.2	11.9	109.4	2.6
Capital Expenditure	(4.4)	(6.8)	(13.0)	(22.5)	(55.0)
Depreciation & Amort.	6.3	9.1	9.1	18.1	23.5
Cash Acquisitions	(38.7)	(154.7)	(132.8)	(320.5)	(3.7)
Amort. of Goodwill and Intangibles	6.1	14.3	30.1	31.3	13.6
Total Current Assets	92.9	82.0	137.1	181.3	173.1
Total Current Liabilities	15.4	70.3	96.2	156.9	163.7
Net Property, Plant & Equipment	19.5	19.9	23.5	81.3	115.5
Goodwill	152.2	951.4	1,054.3	891.0	889.8
Other Intangibles	27.3	170.1	184.2	108.3	102.4
Additional Paid In Capital	333.5	1,153.8	1,217.8	1,393.8	1,432.9
Retained Earnings	(56.4)	(87.5)	(69.8)	(623.3)	(627.4)
Comprehensive Inc. and Other	(2.4)	0.7	(63.4)	(71.1)	(69.2)
Total Common Equity	274.7	1,067.1	1,084.7	693.4	730.2

L-1 Identity Solutions Inc. (NYSE:ID)
In Millions of USD, except per share items.

Cash Flow					
For the Fiscal Period Ending	Dec-31-2005	Dec-31-2006	Restated Dec-31-2007	Restated Dec-31-2008	Dec-31-2009
Net Income	(7.4)	(31.0)	15.8	(551.6)	(4.2)
Depreciation & Amort.	6.3	9.1	9.1	18.1	23.5
Amort. of Goodwill and Intangibles	6.1	14.3	30.1	31.3	13.6
Depreciation & Amort., Total	12.4	23.4	39.2	49.4	37.1

			Cash Flow		
For the Fiscal Period Ending	Dec-31-2005	Dec-31-2006	Restated Dec-31-2007	Restated Dec-31-2008	Dec-31-2009
Other Amortization	—	0.1	4.3	8.7	12.1
(Gain) Loss from Sale of Assets	0	—	—	—	—
Asset Writedown & Restructuring Costs	—	17.4	5.0	528.6	—
Stock-Based Compensation	0.3	8.1	11.3	18.1	23.7
Tax Benefit from Stock Options	—	—	(2.7)	(0.7)	(0.1)
Other Operating Activities	1.1	2.4	(25.8)	7.9	(2.6)
Change in Acc. Receivable	3.0	(20.8)	(9.3)	0.2	(10.0)
Change in Inventories	(1.5)	(0.4)	(9.5)	(7.9)	4.9
Change in Acc. Payable	(5.5)	14.5	11.6	4.8	(0.8)
Change in Unearned Rev.	0.3	0.7	0.4	1.7	(3.9)
Change in Other Net Operating Assets	1.6	(1.7)	0.7	(6.4)	4.4
Cash from Ops.	**4.4**	**12.6**	**41.0**	**52.8**	**60.6**
Capital Expenditure	(4.4)	(6.8)	(13.0)	(22.5)	(55.0)
Sale of Property, Plant & Equipment	0.5	—	—	—	—
Cash Acquisitions	(38.7)	(154.7)	(132.8)	(320.5)	(3.7)
Divestitures	—	—	—	—	—
Sale (Purchase) of Intangible assets	(0.3)	(1.3)	(6.3)	(8.0)	(7.5)
Invest. in Marketable & Equity Securt.	—	—	—	—	—
Net (Inc.) Dec. in Loans Originated/Sold	—	—	—	—	—
Other Investing Activities	—	0.4	0.2	0	0
Cash from Investing	**(42.9)**	**(162.4)**	**(151.9)**	**(350.9)**	**(66.2)**
Short-Term Debt Issued	—	—	—	—	—
Long-Term Debt Issued	0.2	80.0	179.0	295.0	24.9
Total Debt Issued	**0.2**	**80.0**	**179.0**	**295.0**	**24.9**

(Continued)

		Cash Flow		
For the Fiscal Period Ending	Dec-31-2005	Dec-31-2006	Restated Dec-31-2007	Restated Dec-31-2008	Dec-31-2009
Short-Term Debt Repaid	—	—	—	—	—
Long-Term Debt Repaid	(0.3)	(0.3)	(0.8)	(88.8)	(35.1)
Total Debt Repaid	**(0.3)**	**(0.3)**	**(0.8)**	**(88.8)**	**(35.1)**
Issuance of Common Stock	99.6	7.2	11.9	109.4	2.6
Repurchase of Common Stock	—	—	—	(6.2)	—
Issuance of Pref. Stock	—	—	—	15.1	—
Total Dividends Paid	**—**	**—**	**—**	**—**	**—**
Special Dividend Paid	—	—	—	—	—
Other Financing Activities	—	(4.6)	(76.1)	(13.7)	(0.9)
Cash from Financing	**99.6**	**82.3**	**114.1**	**310.8**	**(8.5)**
Foreign Exchange Rate Adj.	0	0.2	0.1	(0.4)	0.3
Net Change in Cash	**61.1**	**(67.4)**	**3.2**	**12.2**	**(13.8)**

AVEO Pharmaceuticals, Inc. (NasdaqGM:AVEO)
In Millions USD, except per share items.

		Balance Sheet		
Balance Sheet as of:	Dec-31-2006	Dec-31-2007	Dec-31-2008	Dec-31-2009	Sep-30-2010
ASSETS					
Cash and Equivalents	—	21.083	20.814	45.289	40.046
Short-Term Investments	—	40.659	11.550	6.011	46.976
Total Cash & ST Investments	**—**	**61.742**	**32.364**	**51.301**	**87.022**
Accounts Receivable	—	0.621	2.081	0.487	0.220
Total Receivables	**—**	**0.621**	**2.081**	**0.487**	**0.22**

	Balance Sheet				
Balance Sheet as of:	Dec-31-2006	Dec-31-2007	Dec-31-2008	Dec-31-2009	Sep-30-2010
Prepaid Exp.	—	0.982	1.162	1.306	3.598
Other Current Assets	—	—	—	—	—
Total Current Assets	—	63.345	35.607	53.094	90.84
Gross Property, Plant & Equipment	—	9.918	11.237	12.971	—
Accumulated Depreciation	—	(6.192)	(7.485)	(8.774)	—
Net Property, Plant & Equipment	—	3.727	3.752	4.197	4.488
Other Long-Term Assets	—	0.582	0.728	2.553	1.184
Total Assets	—	67.654	40.087	59.844	96.512
LIABILITIES					
Accounts Payable	—	2.417	3.854	7.490	8.797
Accrued Exp.	—	2.991	3.409	7.389	9.111
Curr. Port. of LT Debt	—	6.443	5.037	7.467	3.398
Unearned Revenue, Current	—	8.810	7.092	11.782	11.945
Other Current Liabilities	—	0.142	0.141	0.176	0.264
Total Current Liabilities	—	20.803	19.533	34.305	33.515
Long-Term Debt	—	8.635	16.018	12.278	19.742
Unearned Revenue, Non-Current	—	10.937	6.048	23.320	16.736
Other Non-Current Liabilities	—	1.112	2.245	2.069	3.108
Total Liabilities	—	41.488	43.844	71.972	73.101
Pref. Stock, Convertible	—	123.720	123.720	156.705	—
Pref. Stock, Other	—	0.905	1.211	1.459	—
Total Pref. Equity	—	124.625	124.931	158.163	—
Common Stock	—	0.006	0.002	0.002	0.031
Additional Paid In Capital	—	2.579	4.924	7.432	249.580

(*Continued*)

		Balance Sheet			
Balance Sheet as of:	Dec-31-2006	Dec-31-2007	Dec-31-2008	Dec-31-2009	Sep-30-2010
Retained Earnings	—	(101.158)	(133.631)	(177.725)	(226.200)
Treasury Stock	—	—	—	—	—
Comprehensive Inc. and Other	—	0.115	0.018	0	—
Total Common Equity	—	(98.458)	(128.688)	(170.291)	23.411
Total Equity	—	26.167	(3.757)	(12.127)	23.411
Total Liabilities and Equity	—	67.654	40.087	59.844	96.512
Supplemental Items					
Total Shares Out. on Balance Sheet Date	1.33	1.434	1.586	1.641	30.935

AVEO Pharmaceuticals, Inc. (NasdaqGM:AVEO)
In Millions of USD, except per share items.

		Analysis (selected items)			
For the Fiscal Period Ending	Dec-31-2006	Dec-31-2007	Dec-31-2008	Dec-31-2009	12 months Sep-30-2010
Total Revenue	7.783	11.034	19.660	20.719	38.761
Gross Profit	5.452	9.009	16.824	17.759	36.001
Selling General & Admin Exp.	5.161	6.502	9.165	10.120	12.815
R & D Exp.	24.514	27.223	38.985	48.832	79.573
Net Income	(24.905)	(24.982)	(32.473)	(44.093)	(59.191)
Total Cash & ST Investments		61.742	32.364	51.301	87.022
Net Property, Plant & Equipment		3.727	3.752	4.197	4.488
Total Assets		67.654	40.087	59.844	96.512
Total Current Liabilities		20.803	19.533	34.305	33.515
Cash from Ops.	(21.716)	(8.604)	(35.301)	(9.973)	(57.827)
Cash from Investing	18.917	(39.894)	28.151	3.414	(26.947)
Cash from Financing	12.840	52.834	6.881	31.035	84.636

	Analysis (selected items)				
For the Fiscal Period Ending	Dec-31-2006	Dec-31-2007	Dec-31-2008	Dec-31-2009	12 months Sep-30-2010
Total Debt Issued	14.835	—	20.795	—	7.555
Total Debt Repaid	(2.042)	(4.620)	(13.948)	(1.986)	(4.039)
Issuance of Common Stock	0.047	0.078	0.034	0.159	81.120
Issuance of Pref. Stock	—	57.497	—	32.925	0.063
Total Shares Out. on Balance Sheet Date	1.33	1.434	1.586	1.641	30.935

AVEO Pharmaceuticals, Inc. (NasdaqGM:AVEO)
In Millions of USD, except per share items.

	Cash Flow				
For the Fiscal Period Ending	Dec-31-2006	Dec-31-2007	Dec-31-2008	Dec-31-2009	12 months Sep-30-2010
Net Income	(24.905)	(24.982)	(32.473)	(44.093)	(59.191)
Depreciation & Amort.	1.355	1.334	1.321	1.289	1.296
Depreciation & Amort., Total	1.355	1.334	1.321	1.289	1.296
(Gain) Loss from Sale of Assets	—	—	0.010	—	0.001
(Gain) Loss on Sale of Invest.	0.072	(1.025)	(0.496)	0.373	0.198
Stock-Based Compensation	0.243	0.788	2.306	2.387	3.605
Other Operating Activities	0.224	0.541	0.717	1.019	0.662
Change in Acc. Receivable	—	(0.621)	(1.46)	1.594	0.321
Change in Acc. Payable	(0.076)	1.285	1.437	3.636	4.688

(Continued)

	Cash Flow				
For the Fiscal Period Ending	Dec-31-2006	Dec-31-2007	Dec-31-2008	Dec-31-2009	12 months Sep-30-2010
Change in Unearned Rev.	(2.366)	18.329	(6.607)	21.962	(8.350)
Change in Other Net Operating Assets	3.736	(4.254)	(0.056)	1.860	(1.057)
Cash from Ops.	**(21.716)**	**(8.604)**	**(35.301)**	**(9.973)**	**(57.827)**
Capital Expenditure	(0.333)	(0.375)	(1.357)	(1.734)	(1.796)
Cash Acquisitions	—	—	—	—	—
Divestitures	—	—	—	—	—
Invest. in Marketable & Equity Securt.	19.250	(39.519)	29.507	5.148	(25.151)
Net (Inc.) Dec. in Loans Originated/Sold	—	—	—	—	—
Other Investing Activities	—	—	—	—	—
Cash from Investing	**18.917**	**(39.894)**	**28.151**	**3.414**	**(26.947)**
Short-Term Debt Issued	—	—	—	—	—
Long-Term Debt Issued	14.835	—	20.795	—	—
Total Debt Issued	**14.835**	**—**	**20.795**	**—**	**7.555**
Short-Term Debt Repaid	—	—	—	—	—
Long-Term Debt Repaid	(2.042)	(4.620)	(13.948)	(1.986)	—
Total Debt Repaid	**(2.042)**	**(4.620)**	**(13.948)**	**(1.986)**	**(4.039)**
Issuance of Common Stock	0.047	0.078	0.034	0.159	81.120
Issuance of Pref. Stock	—	57.497	—	32.925	0.063
Total Dividends Paid	**—**	**—**	**—**	**—**	**—**
Special Dividend Paid	—	—	—	—	—
Other Financing Activities	—	(0.121)	—	(0.063)	(0.063)
Cash from Financing	**12.840**	**52.834**	**6.881**	**31.035**	**84.636**
Net Change in Cash	**10.040**	**4.335**	**(0.269)**	**24.476**	**(0.138)**

United Therapeutics Corp. (NasdaqGS:UTHR)
In Millions USD, except per share items.

		Balance Sheet			
Balance Sheet as of:	Dec-31-2005	Restated Dec-31-2006	Dec-31-2007	Restated Dec-31-2008	Dec-31-2009
ASSETS					
Cash and Equivalents	69.2	91.1	139.3	129.5	100.4
Short-Term Investments	56.3	136.7	150.7	106.6	129.1
Total Cash & ST Investments	**125.5**	**227.7**	**290.1**	**236.0**	**229.5**
Accounts Receivable	13.9	22.5	25.7	28.3	50.6
Other Receivables	5.1	3.2	4.0	2.3	2.6
Total Receivables	**19.0**	**25.6**	**29.7**	**30.6**	**53.3**
Inventory	11.3	12.0	13.2	14.4	26.4
Prepaid Exp.	6.4	9.2	5.9	11.6	8.2
Deferred Tax Assets, Curr.	4.6	2.7	13.6	4.8	7.2
Other Current Assets	0	—	—	—	—
Total Current Assets	**166.8**	**277.4**	**352.5**	**297.4**	**324.5**
Gross Property, Plant & Equipment	29.4	43.9	79.7	236.5	327.2
Accumulated Depreciation	(7.6)	(9.3)	(10.4)	(13.7)	(23.3)
Net Property, Plant & Equipment	**21.8**	**34.7**	**69.4**	**222.7**	**303.9**
Long-term Investments	53.1	41.1	11.0	108.0	154.4
Goodwill	7.5	7.5	7.5	7.5	8.8
Other Intangibles	5.5	3.1	1.0	0.4	9.7
Loans Receivable Long-Term	0	—	—	—	—
Deferred Tax Assets, LT	15.1	65.3	93.7	178.8	201.0
Other Long-Term Assets	21.7	47.9	52.1	59.7	49.4
Total Assets	**291.4**	**477.0**	**587.0**	**874.5**	**1,051.5**

(*Continued*)

	Balance Sheet				
Balance Sheet as of:	Dec-31-2005	Restated Dec-31-2006	Dec-31-2007	Restated Dec-31-2008	Dec-31-2009
LIABILITIES					
Accounts Payable	4.0	3.1	2.0	20.3	18.8
Accrued Exp.	10.4	15.3	17.9	29.4	29.8
Curr. Port. of LT Debt	—	0	250.0	—	220.3
Curr. Port. of Cap. Leases	0	—	—	—	—
Other Current Liabilities	0.1	0.9	2.8	8.0	61.4
Total Current Liabilities	**14.5**	**19.3**	**272.8**	**57.7**	**330.2**
Long-Term Debt	0	250.0	—	205.7	—
Capital Leases	—	—	—	29.3	30.3
Pension & Other Post-Retire. Benefits	—	—	4.9	9.2	14.5
Other Non-Current Liabilities	1.8	3.1	13.6	17.4	23.5
Total Liabilities	**16.3**	**272.4**	**291.2**	**319.2**	**398.5**
Common Stock	0.2	0.2	0.3	0.3	0.6
Additional Paid In Capital	393.5	408.8	548.3	722.3	798.9
Retained Earnings	(115.3)	(41.4)	(21.5)	(93.9)	(74.7)
Treasury Stock	(6.9)	(164.6)	(231.6)	(67.4)	(67.4)
Comprehensive Inc. and Other	3.6	1.5	0.3	(5.9)	(4.3)
Total Common Equity	**275.1**	**204.6**	**295.8**	**555.3**	**653.0**
Total Equity	**275.1**	**204.6**	**295.8**	**555.3**	**653.0**
Total Liabilities and Equity	**291.4**	**477.0**	**587.0**	**874.5**	**1,051.5**
Supplemental Items					
Total Shares Out. on Balance Sheet Date	46.6	43.0	44.5	52.9	54.2

United Therapeutics Corp. (NasdaqGS:UTHR)
In Millions of USD, except per share items.

	Analysis				
For the Fiscal Period Ending	Restated Dec-31-2005	Restated Dec-31-2006	Restated Dec-31-2007	Restated Dec-31-2008	Dec-31-2009
Total Revenue	115.9	159.6	210.9	281.5	369.8
Gross Profit	103.6	142.6	188.7	251.4	324.5
Selling General & Admin Exp.	24.7	54.0	99.0	91.2	172.1
R & D Exp.	36.1	57.6	83.4	89.2	122.2
Net Income	65.0	74.0	12.4	(49.3)	19.5
Cash from Ops.	43.2	49.3	48.9	(49.2)	97.6
Cash from Investing	(70.7)	(101.6)	(21.7)	(172.5)	(160.5)
Cash from Financing	14.2	74.1	20.9	213.0	36.5
Capital Expenditure	(6.1)	(15.6)	(38.7)	(124.4)	(95.4)
Depreciation & Amort.	2.1	2.4	2.9	3.9	10.7
Cash Acquisitions	—	—	—	—	(3.6)
Total Debt Issued	—	242.0	—	—	—
Issuance of Common Stock	15.0	14.4	58.3	191.9	32.1
Repurchase of Common Stock	—	(157.7)	(67.1)	—	—
Stock-Based Compensation	1.0	24.1	48.7	28.7	101.0
Tax Benefit from Stock Options	—	(10.8)	(29.6)	(21.1)	(4.4)

United Therapeutics Corp. (NasdaqGS:UTHR)
In Millions of USD, except per share items.

	Cash Flow				
For the Fiscal Period Ending	Restated Dec-31-2005	Restated Dec-31-2006	Restated Dec-31-2007	Restated Dec-31-2008	Dec-31-2009
Net Income	65.0	74.0	12.4	(49.3)	19.5
Depreciation & Amort.	2.1	2.4	2.9	3.9	10.7
Amort. of Goodwill and Intangibles	0.5	0.3	0.5	0.6	0.7
Depreciation & Amort., Total	2.5	2.7	3.4	4.5	11.4

(Continued)

| | Cash Flow | | | | |
For the Fiscal Period Ending	Restated Dec-31-2005	Restated Dec-31-2006	Restated Dec-31-2007	Restated Dec-31-2008	Dec-31-2009
Other Amortization	—	—	13.7	14.7	15.7
(Gain) Loss from Sale of Assets	0.1	—	—	—	—
(Gain) Loss on Sale of Invest.	(0.1)	0.8	(0.5)	0.6	6.0
(Income) Loss on Equity Invest.	0.8	0.6	1.5	(2.5)	(1.8)
Stock-Based Compensation	1.0	24.1	48.7	28.7	101.0
Tax Benefit from Stock Options	—	(10.8)	(29.6)	(21.1)	(4.4)
Provision & Write-Off of Bad Debts	0.1	0.3	2.0	0.6	4.7
Other Operating Activities	(17.9)	(37.0)	3.1	(34.4)	(1.0)
Change in Acc. Receivable	(0.2)	(8.9)	(4.0)	(2.3)	(22.0)
Change in Inventories	(3.5)	(1.0)	(2.3)	(2.6)	(9.1)
Change in Acc. Payable	(2.1)	(1.1)	(1.1)	18.5	(3.6)
Change in Other Net Operating Assets	(2.4)	5.7	1.6	(4.5)	(18.7)
Cash from Ops.	43.2	49.3	48.9	(49.2)	97.6
Capital Expenditure	(6.1)	(15.6)	(38.7)	(124.4)	(95.4)
Cash Acquisitions	—	—	—	—	(3.6)
Divestitures	—	—	—	—	—
Invest. in Marketable & Equity Securt.	(64.6)	(86.0)	17.0	(48.1)	(61.6)
Net (Inc.) Dec. in Loans Originated/Sold	—	—	—	—	—
Other Investing Activities	—	—	—	—	—
Cash from Investing	(70.7)	(101.6)	(21.7)	(172.5)	(160.5)
Short-Term Debt Issued	—	—	—	—	—
Long-Term Debt Issued	—	242.0	—	—	—
Total Debt Issued	—	242.0	—	—	—
Short-Term Debt Repaid	—	—	—	—	—
Long-Term Debt Repaid	(0.8)	0	—	—	—
Total Debt Repaid	(0.8)	0	—	—	—

For the Fiscal Period Ending	Cash Flow				
	Restated Dec-31-2005	Restated Dec-31-2006	Restated Dec-31-2007	Restated Dec-31-2008	Dec-31-2009
Issuance of Common Stock	15.0	14.4	58.3	191.9	32.1
Repurchase of Common Stock	—	(157.7)	(67.1)	—	—
Total Dividends Paid	—	—	—	—	—
Special Dividend Paid	—	—	—	—	—
Other Financing Activities	—	(24.6)	29.6	21.1	4.4
Cash from Financing	14.2	74.1	20.9	213.0	36.5
Foreign Exchange Rate Adj.	—	0.1	0.1	(1.2)	(2.7)
Net Change in Cash	(13.4)	21.9	48.3	(9.9)	(29.1)

5. Perform a Du Pont analysis for the firms in the table below.

Du Pont Analysis of Packaged Foods and Meats 2009

Company Name	Sales	Total Assets	Net Income (Loss)	Total Equity
Campbell Soup Co. (NYSE:CPB)	7,570.0	6,152.0	806.0	1,023.0
ConAgra Foods, Inc. (NYSE:CAG)	12,176.8	11,566.5	773.5	4,984.6
Dean Foods Co. (NYSE:DF)	11,158.4	7,843.9	240.3	1,351.9
General Mills Inc. (NYSE:GIS)	14,743.7	18,561.3	1,633.8	6,088.9
Hershey Co. (NYSE:HSY)	5,298.7	3,675.0	436.0	720.5
HJ Heinz Co. (NYSE:HNZ)	10,262.5	10,071.2	847.7	1,823.7
Hormel Foods Corp. (NYSE:HRL)	6,572.0	3,730.7	372.6	2,209.9
Kellogg Company (NYSE:K)	12,575.0	11,200.0	1,212.0	2,272.0
Kraft Foods Inc. (NYSE:KFT)	40,386.0	66,714.0	3,021.0	25,876.0
McCormick & Co. Inc. (NYSE:MKC)	3,192.1	3,387.8	299.8	1,334.6
Mead Johnson Nutrition Company (NYSE:MJN)	2,826.5	2,070.3	399.6	(674.9)
Sara Lee Corp. (NYSE:SLE)	12,677.0	9,930.0	806.0	2,753.0
The J. M. Smucker Company (NYSE:SJM)	4,604.8	7,899.4	467.8	5,240.2
Tyson Foods Inc. (NYSE:TSN)	26,818.0	10,851.0	(275.0)	4,543.0

6. Using the information in the financial statements of Advanced Battery Technologies to calculate the following ratios:

Advanced Battery Technologies, Inc. (NasdaqCM:ABAT)
Ratios (except as noted)

For the Fiscal Period Ending	Dec-31- 2005	Dec-31- 2006	Dec-31- 2007	Dec-31- 2008	Dec-31- 2009
PROFITABILITY					
Return on Assets %					
Return on Capital %					
Return on Equity %					
Return on Common Equity %					
Gross Margin %					
SG&A Margin %					
EBITDA Margin %					
EBITA Margin %					
EBIT Margin %					
Earnings from Cont. Ops Margin %					
Net Income Margin %					
ACTIVITY					
Total Asset Turnover					
Fixed Asset Turnover					
Receivable Turnover					
Inventory Turnover					
LIQUIDITY					
Current Ratio					
Quick Ratio					
Avg. Days Sales Out.					
Avg. Days Inventory Out.					
Avg. Days Payable Out.					
Avg. Cash Conversion Cycle					
LEVERAGE					
Total Debt/Equity					
Total Debt/Capital					
LT Debt/Equity					
LT Debt/Capital					
Total Liabilities/Total Assets					

For the Fiscal Period Ending	Dec-31-2005	Dec-31-2006	Dec-31-2007	Dec-31-2008	Dec-31-2009
COVERAGE					
EBIT/Interest Exp.					
EBITDA/Interest Exp.					
(EBITDA-CAPEX)/Interest Exp.					
Total Debt/EBITDA					
Net Debt/EBITDA					
Total Debt/(EBITDA-CAPEX)					
Net Debt/(EBITDA-CAPEX)					

Advanced Battery Technologies, Inc. (NasdaqCM:ABAT)
In Millions of USD, except per share items.

Balance Sheet	Dec-31-2005	Restated Dec-31-2006	Dec-31-2007	Dec-31-2008	Dec-31-2009
ASSETS					
Cash and Equivalents	0	0	2.7	32.7	52.9
Total Cash & ST Investments	0	0	2.7	32.7	52.9
Accounts Receivable	2.0	4.9	16.0	14.7	22.4
Other Receivables	—	0.7	0.1	0.2	0.1
Notes Receivable	—	0.9	—	1.6	1.6
Total Receivables	2.0	6.5	16.1	16.5	24.1
Inventory	0.4	0.4	1.2	1.7	3.7
Prepaid Exp.	0.9	—	—	—	—
Other Current Assets	—	1.0	1.6	0.2	7.9
Total Current Assets	3.3	8.0	21.6	51.3	88.7
Gross Property, Plant & Equipment	12.7	—	15.3	19.4	57.7
Accumulated Depreciation	(0.8)	—	(2.0)	(2.8)	(10.5)
Net Property, Plant & Equipment	11.9	12.9	13.2	16.6	47.2
Long-Term Investments	—	—	—	1.0	0.8
Goodwill	—	2.2	2.3	2.5	2.5
Other Intangibles	0.5	1.5	1.6	1.5	14.3
Other Long-Term Assets	1.5	—	0	4.8	4.3
Total Assets	17.2	24.6	38.7	77.8	157.8

(*Continued*)

Balance Sheet	Dec-31-2005	Restated Dec-31-2006	Dec-31-2007	Dec-31-2008	Dec-31-2009
LIABILITIES					
Accounts Payable	1.0	0.6	0.4	0.4	0.7
Accrued Exp.	1.0	0.3	0.6	0.8	1.4
Short-Term Borrowings	4.1	—	0.7	0	2.9
Unearned Revenue, Current	0.1	0	0.1	0.1	0.2
Other Current Liabilities	—	—	—	—	—
Total Current Liabilities	**6.2**	**1.0**	**1.8**	**1.3**	**5.2**
Long-Term Debt	—	0.4	0.4	—	—
Minority Interest	1.9	—	—	—	—
Def. Tax Liability, Non-Curr.	—	—	—	—	3.5
Other Non-Current Liabilities	—	—	—	—	17.2
Total Liabilities	**8.1**	**1.4**	**2.2**	**1.3**	**25.9**
Common Stock	0	0	0	0.1	0.1
Additional Paid in Capital	13.8	17.1	18.0	39.3	74.1
Retained Earnings	(2.9)	5.1	15.3	31.4	52.8
Treasury Stock	—	—	—	(0.3)	(0.5)
Comprehensive Inc. and Other	(1.8)	1.0	3.1	6.0	5.5
Total Common Equity	**9.1**	**23.2**	**36.5**	**76.5**	**131.9**
Total Equity	**9.1**	**23.2**	**36.5**	**76.5**	**131.9**
Total Liabilities and Equity	**17.2**	**24.6**	**38.7**	**77.8**	**157.8**

Advanced Battery Technologies, Inc. (NasdaqCM:ABAT)
In Millions of USD, except per share items.

	Income Statement				
For the Fiscal Period Ending	Reclassified Dec-31-2005	Dec-31-2006	Reclassified Dec-31-2007	Dec-31-2008	Dec-31-2009
Revenue	4.2	16.3	31.9	45.2	63.6
Other Revenue	—	—	—	—	—
Total Revenue	**4.2**	**16.3**	**31.9**	**45.2**	**63.6**
Cost of Goods Sold	2.8	7.3	18.0	23.1	35.2
Gross Profit	**1.4**	**9.0**	**13.9**	**22.0**	**28.4**

Income Statement

For the Fiscal Period Ending	Reclassified Dec-31-2005	Dec-31-2006	Reclassified Dec-31-2007	Dec-31-2008	Dec-31-2009
Selling General & Admin Exp.	1.3	1.4	2.4	3.3	11.2
R & D Exp.	—	0.2	0.4	0	0.3
Depreciation & Amort.	—	—	—	—	—
Other Operating Expense/(Income)	—	—	—	—	—
Other Operating Exp., Total	**1.3**	**1.6**	**2.8**	**3.3**	**11.5**
Operating Income	**0.1**	**7.4**	**11.1**	**18.8**	**16.9**
Interest Expense	(0.2)	(0.2)	—	—	(0.5)
Interest and Invest. Income	—	—	0	0.1	0.3
Net Interest Exp.	**(0.2)**	**(0.2)**	**0**	**0.1**	**(0.2)**
Income/(Loss) from Affiliates	—	—	—	(0.1)	0
Other Non-Operating Inc. (Exp.)	0.1	0	—	0	0
EBT Excl. Unusual Items	**0**	**7.1**	**11.1**	**18.8**	**16.7**
Impairment of Goodwill	—	—	—	—	9.9
Other Unusual Items	—	—	(0.9)	—	1.0
EBT Incl. Unusual Items	**0**	**7.1**	**10.2**	**18.8**	**27.6**
Income Tax Expense	—	(0.9)	—	2.7	6.2
Minority Int. in Earnings	(0.2)	—	—	—	—
Earnings from Cont. Ops.	**(0.2)**	**8.0**	**10.2**	**16.1**	**21.4**
Earnings of Discontinued Ops.	—	—	—	—	—
Extraord. Item & Account. Change	—	—	—	—	—
Net Income	**(0.2)**	**8.0**	**10.2**	**16.1**	**21.4**
Supplemental Items					
EBITDA	0.7	7.9	11.8	19.5	19.5
EBITA	0.2	7.5	11.2	18.9	17.5
EBIT	0.1	7.4	11.1	18.8	16.9

Advanced Battery Technologies, Inc. (NasdaqCM:ABAT)
In Millions of USD, except per share items.

	Cash Flow				
For the Fiscal Period Ending	12 months Dec-31-2005	Restated 12 months Dec-31-2006	12 months Dec-31-2007	Restated 12 months Dec-31-2008	12 months Dec-31-2009
Net Income	(0.2)	8.0	10.2	16.1	21.4
Depreciation & Amort.	0.5	0.4	0.6	0.6	2.0
Amort. of Goodwill and Intangibles	0	0.1	0.1	0.1	0.6
Depreciation & Amort., Total	0.5	0.5	0.7	0.8	2.6
Other Amortization	—	0.4	—	—	—
(Gain) Loss from Sale of Assets	—	—	—	0.1	—
(Gain) Loss on Sale of Invest.	—	—	—	0.4	0.2
Asset Writedown & Restructuring Costs	—	—	—	—	(9.9)
(Income) Loss on Equity Invest.	—	—	—	0.1	0
Stock-Based Compensation	0.5	0.4	0.9	0.9	2.1
Provision & Write-Off of Bad Debts	—	—	—	0.1	(0.2)
Minority Int. in Earnings	0.2	—	—	—	—
Other Operating Activities	—	0	0.8	—	2.5
Change in Acc. Receivable	(1.9)	(3.0)	(11.1)	1.0	(6.5)
Change in Inventories	(0.1)	0	(0.7)	(0.6)	(0.3)
Change in Acc. Payable	1.5	(1.0)	(0.3)	0.2	(7.8)
Change in Unearned Rev.	(0.7)	(0.1)	0	0	(1.2)
Change in Inc. Taxes	—	—	—	—	(0.2)
Change in Other Net Operating Assets	(0.5)	(0.8)	0	1.5	(5.6)
Cash from Ops.	(0.8)	4.4	0.6	20.4	(2.9)

	Cash Flow				
For the Fiscal Period Ending	12 months Dec-31- 2005	Restated 12 months Dec-31- 2006	12 months Dec-31- 2007	Restated 12 months Dec-31- 2008	12 months Dec-31- 2009
Capital Expenditure	(2.5)	(0.1)	(0.1)	(3.2)	(9.3)
Sale of Property, Plant & Equipment	—	—	—	—	—
Cash Acquisitions	—	—	—	(3.0)	(0.6)
Divestitures	—	—	—	—	—
Invest. in Marketable & Equity Securt.	—	—	—	(1.5)	—
Net (Inc.) Dec. in Loans Originated/Sold	—	—	—	(1.6)	—
Other Investing Activities	—	—	—	(1.7)	(2.8)
Cash from Investing	(2.5)	(0.1)	(0.1)	(11.0)	(12.8)
Short-Term Debt Issued	—	—	0.8	—	—
Long-Term Debt Issued	0.9	—	—	—	—
Total Debt Issued	0.9	—	0.8	—	—
Short-Term Debt Repaid	—	—	—	(0.7)	(4.5)
Long-Term Debt Repaid	0	(3.7)	—	(0.4)	—
Total Debt Repaid	0	(3.7)	—	(1.1)	(4.5)
Issuance of Common Stock	—	—	—	20.4	40.8
Repurchase of Common Stock	—	—	—	(0.3)	(0.2)
Repurchase of Preferred Stock	—	—	—	—	—
Total Dividends Paid	—	—	—	—	—
Special Dividend Paid	—	—	—	—	—
Other Financing Activities	1.7	(0.9)	—	—	—
Cash from Financing	2.6	(4.6)	0.8	18.9	36.1
Foreign Exchange Rate Adj.	0	0.3	1.4	1.7	(0.2)
Net Change in Cash	(0.7)	0	2.7	30.0	20.2

Computational Exercises

THE ARITHMETIC OF GROWTH VALUATIONS

Using a simple framework we call "the arithmetic of growth valuations," we explore the consequences for the owner's wealth of changes in expectations regarding the corporation's earnings growth. We provide four numerical examples to illustrate this point. The reader will be well served by coming back to these simple examples and work through the consequences of the strategies and schemes presented throughout the book.

Case 1

A corporation is currently reporting annual net earnings of $30.0 million. Assume that five years from now, when its growth has leveled off somewhat, the corporation will be valued at 15 times earnings.

Further assume that the company will pay no dividends over the next five years and that investors in growth stocks currently seek returns of 25 percent (before considering capital gains taxes). Suppose the corporation's earnings have been growing at a 15 percent annual rate and appear likely to continue increasing at the same rate over the next five years.

At the end of that period, earnings (rounded) will be $_____$ million annually. Applying a multiple of 15 times to that figure produces a valuation at the end of the fifth year of $_____$ million. Investors seeking a 25 percent rate of return will pay $_____$ million today for that future value.

Say the founder still owns 20 percent of the shares outstanding, which means she is worth $_____$ million. Suppose investors conclude for some reason that the corporation's potential for increasing its earnings has changed from 15 to 25 percent per annum.

The value of corporation's shares will change from $_____$ million to $_____$ million, keeping previous assumptions intact. Now the founder's shares are worth $_____$ million, a difference of $_____$.

Case 2

A corporation is currently reporting annual net earnings of $20.0 million. Assume that five years from now, when its growth has leveled off somewhat, the corporation will be valued at 20 times earnings.

Further assume that the company will pay no dividends over the next five years and that investors in growth stocks currently seek returns of 22 percent (before considering capital gains taxes). Suppose the corporation's earnings have been growing at a 20 percent annual rate and appear likely to continue increasing at the same rate over the next five years.

At the end of that period, earnings (rounded) will be $_____ million annually. Applying a multiple of 20 times to that figure produces a valuation at the end of the fifth year of $_____ million. Investors seeking a 22 percent rate of return will pay $_____ million today for that future value.

Say the founder still owns 40 percent of the shares outstanding, which means she is worth $_____ million. Suppose investors conclude for some reason that the corporation's potential for increasing its earnings has changed from 20 to 18 percent per annum.

The value of corporation's shares will change from $_____ million to $_____ million, keeping previous assumptions intact. Now the founder's shares are worth $_____ million, a difference of $_____.

Case 3

A corporation is currently reporting annual net earnings of $20.0 million. Assume that five years from now, when its growth has leveled off somewhat, the corporation will be valued at 12 times earnings.

Further assume that the company will pay no dividends over the next five years and that investors in growth stocks currently seek returns of 25 percent (before considering capital gains taxes). Suppose the corporation's earnings have been growing at a 10 percent annual rate and appear likely to continue increasing at the same rate over the next five years.

At the end of that period, earnings (rounded) will be $_____ million annually. Applying a multiple of 12 times to that figure produces a valuation at the end of the fifth year of $_____ million. Investors seeking a 25 percent rate of return will pay $_____ million today for that future value.

Say the founder still owns 20 percent of the shares outstanding, which means she is worth $_____ million. Suppose investors conclude for some reason that the corporation's potential for increasing its earnings has changed from 10 to 20 percent per annum.

The value of corporation's shares will change from $ _____ million to $ _____ million, keeping previous assumptions intact. Now the founder's shares are worth $ _____ million, a difference of $ _____ .

Case 4

A corporation is currently reporting annual net earnings of $20.0 million. Assume that five years from now, when its growth has leveled off somewhat, the corporation will be valued at 20 times earnings.

Further assume that the company will pay no dividends over the next five years and that investors in growth stocks currently seek returns of 22 percent (before considering capital gains taxes). Suppose the corporation's earnings have been growing at a 12 percent annual rate and appear likely to continue increasing at the same rate over the next five years.

At the end of that period, earnings (rounded) will be $ _____ million annually. Applying a multiple of 20 times to that figure produces a valuation at the end of the fifth year of $ _____ million. Investors seeking a 22 percent rate of return will pay $ _____ million today for that future value.

Say the founder still owns 40 percent of the shares outstanding, which means she is worth $ _____ million. Suppose investors conclude for some reason that the corporation's potential for increasing its earnings has changed from 12 to 18 percent per annum.

The value of corporation's shares will change from $ _____ million to $ _____ million, keeping previous assumptions intact. Now the founder's shares are worth $ _____ million, a difference of $ _____ .

MARKET VALUE VERSUS BOOK VALUE OF BONDS

This is an example of how a liability can be an asset. Long-term bonds that are carried in the books at face value in the liability side of the balance sheet, are in fact an asset when their market value is above their face value; on the other hand, when the market value of a bond is below its book value, the bonds represent a larger liability than accounted for in the balance sheet.

Case 1

A firm shows in its books bonds with a face value of $20,000,000. The bonds were issued at par, with a semiannual coupon rate of 12.125 percent, and now have eight years to maturity. However, the bonds are now priced to yield 15.730 percent. The market value of this long-term obligation is

$_____ and the difference between the market value and the book value of the bond is $_____.

Case 2

A firm shows in its books bonds with a face value of $50,000,000. The bonds were issued at par, with a semi-annual coupon rate of 14.125 percent, and now have eight years to maturity. However, the bonds are now priced to yield 10.500 percent. The market value of this long-term obligation is $_____, and the difference between the market value and the book value of the bond is $_____.

Case 3

A firm shows in its books bonds with a face value of $35,000,000. The bonds were issued at par, with a semi-annual coupon rate of 6.000 percent, and now have eight years to maturity. However, the bonds are now priced to yield 10.000 percent. The market value of this long-term obligation is $_____, and the difference between the market value and the book value of the bond is $_____.

ACQUISITIONS DRIVEN BY P/E MULTIPLES

Management can boost sales through techniques that more properly fall into the category of corporate finance. Increasing the rate of revenue increases through mergers and acquisitions is the most common example. A corporation can easily accelerate its sales growth by buying other companies and adding their sales to its own. Creating genuine value for shareholders through acquisitions is more difficult, although unwary investors sometimes fail to recognize the distinction.

In the following fictitious examples, Big Time Corp. is set to acquire Small Change, a smaller, privately owned company in the same industry. What will be the impact of a stock-for-stock transaction on the price-per-share of Big Corp?

Case 1

Big Time Corp.'s sales increase by 10.0 percent between Year 1 and Year 2. Small Change, a smaller, privately owned company in the same industry, also achieves 10.0 percent year-over-year sales growth. Suppose now that at the end of Year 1, Big Time acquires Small Change with shares of its own stock. The Big Time income statements under this assumption ("Acquisition Scenario") show a _____ sales increase between Year 1 and Year 2.

On the face of it, a company growing at _____ a year is sexier than one growing at only 10.0 percent a year. Observe, however, that Big Time's profitability, measured by net income as a percentage of sales, does not improve as a result of the acquisition. Combining two companies with equivalent profit margins of _____ produces a larger company that earns _____ on sales.

If Big Time decides not to acquire Small Change, its number of shares outstanding remains at 125.0 million. The earnings increase from $_____ million in Year 1 to $_____ million in Year 2 raises earnings-per-share from $_____ to $_____. With the price-earnings multiple at _____ times, equivalent to the average of the company's industry peers, Big Time's stock price rises from $_____ to $_____ a share.

In the Acquisition Scenario, on the other hand, Big Time pays its industry-average earnings multiple of 12 times for Small Change, for a total acquisition price of million. At Big Time's Year 1 share price of $_____, the purchase therefore requires the issuance of million shares.

Acquisitions Driven by P/E Multiples
Big Time Corp. and Small Change Inc.

Debt		$1,000.0	32.0
Equity		$1,000.0	25.0
Big Time Annual Coupon Rate for Debt	10%		
Small Change Annual Coupon Rate for Debt	15%		
($000.000) Omitted			

	Non-Acquisition Scenario		Acquisition Scenario
	Big Time Corp.	Small Change Inc.	Big Time Corp.
	Year 1 Year 2	Year 1 Year 2	Year 1 Year 2
Sales	$5,000.0	$238.1	$5,000.0
Cost and Expenses			
Cost of Goods Sold	3,422.7	160.6	3,422.7
Selling, General, and Administrative Expenses	1,250.0	61.9	1,250.0

(Continued)

	Non-Acquisition Scenario				Acquisition Scenario	
	Big Time Corp.		Small Change Inc.		Big Time Corp.	
	Year 1	Year 2	Year 1	Year 2	Year 1	Year 2
Interest Expense	100.0		4.8		100.0	
Total Costs and Expenses	4,772.7		227.3		4,772.7	
Income before Income Tax Expenses	227.3		10.8		227.3	
Income Taxes	77.3		3.7		77.3	
Net Income						
Year-over-Year Sales Increase	150.0		7.1		150.0	
Net Income as a Percentage of Sales	3.0%		3.0%		3.0%	
Shares Outstanding (million)	125.0				125.0	
Earnings per Share						
Price-Earnings Multiple (times)						
Price per Share						
Year-over-Year Increase						
Market Capitalization						
Year-over-Year Increase						
Debt/Equity Ratio						
Acquisition Price						
Number of Shares						
taxrate	34%					
growth_rate	10%					
industry_PE_mult	12					

With the addition of Small Change's net income, Big Time earns $_____ million in Year 2. Dividing that figure by the increased number of shares outstanding (_____ million) produces earnings per share of $_____. At a price-earnings multiple of 12 times, Big Time is worth $_____ a share, precisely the price calculated in the Non-Acquisition Scenario.

The mere increase in annual sales growth from _____ percent to _____ percent has not benefited shareholders, whose shares increase in value by _____ percent whether Big Time acquires Small Change or not.

Case 2

Big Time Corp.'s sales increase by 8.0 percent between Year 1 and Year 2. Small Change, a smaller, privately owned company in the same industry, also achieves 8.0 percent year-over-year sales growth. Suppose now that at the end of Year 1, Big Time acquires Small Change with shares of its own stock. The Big Time income statements under this assumption ("Acquisition Scenario") show a _____ percent sales increase between Year 1 and Year 2.

On the face of it, a company growing at _____ percent a year is sexier than one growing at only 8.0 percent a year. Observe, however, that Big Time's profitability, measured by net income as a percentage of sales, does not improve as a result of the acquisition. Combining two companies with equivalent profit margins of _____ percent produces a larger company that also earns _____ percent on sales. Shareholders do not gain anything in the process, as the figures below demonstrate.

If Big Time decides not to acquire Small Change, its number of shares outstanding remains at 125.0 million. The earnings increase from $_____ million in Year 1 to $_____ million in Year 2 raises earnings-per-share from $_____ to $_____. With the price-earnings multiple at 16 times, equivalent to the average of the company's industry peers, Big Time's stock price rises from $_____ to $_____ a share.

Acquisitions Driven by P/E Multiples
Big Time Corp. and Small Change Inc.

Debt	$1,000.0	32.0	$1,000
Equity	$1,000.0	25.0	$1,000
Big Time Annual Coupon Rate for Debt	10%		
Small Change Annual Coupon Rate for Debt	15%		
($000.000) Omitted			

	Non-Acquisition Scenario				Acquisition Scenario	
	Big Time Corp.		Small Change Inc.		Big Time Corp.	
	Year 1	Year 2	Year 1	Year 2	Year 1	Year 2
Sales	$5,000.0		$238.1		$5,000.0	
Cost and Expenses						
Cost of Goods Sold	3,422.7		160.6		$3,422.7	

(Continued)

	Non-Acquisition Scenario				Acquisition Scenario	
	Big Time Corp.		Small Change Inc.		Big Time Corp.	
	Year 1	Year 2	Year 1	Year 2	Year 1	Year 2
Selling, General, and Administrative Expenses	1250.0		61.9		1,250.0	
Interest Expense	100.0		4.8		100.0	
Total Costs and Expenses	4,772.7		227.3		4,772.7	
Income before Income Tax Expenses	227.3		10.8		227.3	
Income Taxes	77.3		3.7		77.3	
Net Income						
Year-over-Year Sales Increase	150.0		7.1		150.0	
Net Income as a Percentage of Sales	3.0%		3.0%		3.0%	
Shares Outstanding (million)	125.0				125.0	
Earnings per Share						
Price-Earnings Multiple (times)						
Price per Share						
Year-over-Year Increase						
Market Capitalization						
Year-over-Year Increase						
Debt/Equity Ratio						
Acquisition Price						
Number of Shares						
taxrate	34%					
growth_rate	8%					
industry_PE_mult	16					

In the Acquisition Scenario, on the other hand, Big Time pays its industry-average earnings multiple of 16 times for Small Change, for a total acquisition price of $_____ million. At Big Time's Year 1 share price of $_____, the purchase therefore requires the issuance of $_____ million shares. With the addition of Small Change's net income, Big Time earns $_____ million in Year 2. Dividing that figure by the increased number of shares outstanding (_____ million) produces earnings per share of $_____. At a price-earnings multiple of 16 times, Big Time is worth $ _____ a share, precisely the price calculated in the Non-Acquisition Scenario.

The mere increase in annual sales growth from 8.0 percent to _____ percent has not benefited shareholders, whose shares increase in value by _____ percent whether Big Time acquires Small Change or not.

Case 3

Big Time Corp.'s sales increase by 16.0 percent between Year 1 and Year 2. Small Change, a smaller, privately owned company in the same industry, also achieves 16.0 percent year-over-year sales growth. Suppose now that at the end of Year 1, Big Time acquires Small Change with shares of its own stock. The Big Time income statements under this assumption ("Acquisition Scenario") show a _____ percent sales increase between Year 1 and Year 2.

On the face of it, a company growing at _____ percent a year is sexier than one growing at only 16.0 percent a year. Observe, however, that Big Time's profitability, measured by net income as a percentage of sales, does not improve as a result of the acquisition. Combining two companies with equivalent profit margins of _____ percent produces a larger company that also earns _____ percent on sales. Shareholders do not gain anything in the process, as the figures below demonstrate.

If Big Time decides not to acquire Small Change, its number of shares outstanding remains at 125.0 million. The earnings increase from $ _____ million in Year 1 to $ _____ million in Year 2 raises earnings-per-share from $ _____ to $ _____. With the price-earnings multiple at 24 times, equivalent to the average of the company's industry peers, Big Time's stock price rises from $ _____ to $ _____ a share.

Acquisitions Driven by P/E Multiples
Big Time Corp. and Small Change Inc.

Debt	$1,000.0	32.0	$1,000.0
Equity	$1,000.0	25.0	$1,000.0
Big Time Annual Coupon Rate for Debt	10%		
Small Change Annual Coupon Rate for Debt	15%		
($000.000) Omitted			

(Continued)

| | Non-Acquisition Scenario | | | | Acquisition Scenario | |
| | Big Time Corp. | | Small Change Inc. | | Big Time Corp. | |
	Year 1	Year 2	Year 1	Year 2	Year 1	Year 2
Sales	$5,000.0		$238.1		$5,000.0	
Cost and Expenses						
Cost of Goods Sold	3,422.7		160.6		3,422.7	
Selling, General, and Administrative Expenses	1250.0		61.9		1,250.0	
Interest Expense	100.0		4.8		100.0	
Total Costs and Expenses	4,772.7		227.3		4,772.7	
Income before Income Tax Expenses	227.3		10.8		227.3	
Income Taxes	77.3		3.7		77.3	
Net Income						
Year-over-Year Sales Increase	150.0		7.1		150.0	
Net Income as a Percentage of Sales	3.0%		3.0%		3.0%	
Shares Outstanding (million)	125.0				125.0	
Earnings per Share						
Price-Earnings Multiple (times)						
Price per Share						
Year-over-Year Increase						
Market Capitalization						
Year-over-Year Increase						
Debt/Equity Ratio						
Acquisition Price						
Number of Shares						
taxrate	34%					
growth_rate	16%					
industry_PE_mult	24					

In the Acquisition Scenario, on the other hand, Big Time pays its industry-average earnings multiple of 24 times for Small Change, for a total acquisition price of million. At Big Time's Year 1 share price of $_____, the purchase therefore requires the issuance of million shares. With the addition of Small Change's net income, Big Time earns $_____ million in Year 2. Dividing that figure by the increased number of shares outstanding (_____ million) produces earnings per share of $_____. At a price-earnings multiple of 24 times, Big Time is worth $_____ a share, precisely the price calculated in the Non-Acquisition Scenario.

The mere increase in annual sales growth from 16.0 percent to _____ percent has not benefited shareholders, whose shares increase in value by _____ percent whether Big Time acquires Small Change or not.

STOCK PRICES AND GOODWILL

Including goodwill in the calculations of the ratio of Total Assets to Total Liabilities can distort the economic reality of the consequences of acquisitions.

Case 1

The shares of Amalgamator and Consolidator are both trading at multiples of 2.5 times book value per share. Shareholders' equity is $200 million at Amalgamator and $60 million at Consolidator. Amalgamator uses stock held in its treasury to acquire Consolidator for $_____ million.

The purchase price represents a premium of 75 percent above the prevailing market price. Prior to the acquisition, Amalgamator's ratio of total assets to total liabilities is _____ times, while the comparable figure for Consolidator is _____ times.

The total-assets-to-total-liabilities ratio after the deal is _____ times. By paying a premium to Consolidator's tangible asset value, Amalgamator creates $_____ million of goodwill.

	United Amalgamators Corporation	United Consolidators Inc.	Purchase Price	Combined Companies Pro Forma*
Case 1				
Tangible Assets	1,000	400		1,400
Intangible Assets (Goodwill)	0	0		
Total Assets	1,000	400		1,603
Liabilities	800	340		1,140
			Premium	75%

(Continued)

	United Amalgamators Corporation	United Consolidators Inc.	Purchase Price	Combined Companies Pro Forma*		
Stockholder Equity (SE)	200	60				
Total Liabilities and Shareholders' Equity	1,000	400		1,603		
					Multiple	2.5
Total Assets/ Total Liabilities						
Tangible Assets/ Total Liabilities						
Market Capitalization						
Case 2						
Tangible Assets	1,000	400		1,400		
Intangible Assets (Goodwill)	0	0				
Total Assets	1,000	400		1,813		
					Premium	75%
Liabilities	800	340		1,140		
Shareholders' Equity (SE)	200	60				
Total Liabilities and SE	1,000	400		1,813		
					Rally Multiple	4.5
Total Assets/ Total Liabilities						
Tangible Assets/ Total Liabilities						
Market Capitalization						

*Ignores possible impact of EPS dilution.

Case 2

As the scene opens, an explosive stock market rally has driven up both companies' shares to 4.5 times book value. The ratio of total assets to total liabilities, however, remains at _____ times for Amalgamator and _____ times for Consolidator. As in Case 1, Amalgamator pays a premium of 75 percent above the prevailing market price to acquire Consolidator.

The premium is calculated on a higher market capitalization, however. Consequently, the purchase price rises from $_____ million to $_____ million. Instead of creating $_____ million of goodwill, the acquisition gives rise to a $_____ million intangible asset. Somehow, putting together a company boasting a _____ times ratio with another sporting a _____ times ratio has produced an entity with a ratio of _____ times.

Now, let us exclude goodwill in calculating the ratio of assets to liabilities. Amalgamator's ratio of tangible assets to total liabilities following its acquisition of Consolidator is _____ times in both Case 1 and Case 2. This is the outcome that best reflects economic reality.

Case 3

The shares of Amalgamator and Consolidator are both trading at multiples of 1.5 times book value per share. Shareholders' equity is $400 million at Amalgamator and $260 million at Consolidator. Amalgamator uses stock held in its treasury to acquire Consolidator for _____ million.

The purchase price represents a premium of 35.00 percent above the prevailing market price. Prior to the acquisition, Amalgamator's ratio of total assets to total liabilities is _____ times, while the comparable figure for Consolidator is _____ times.

The total-assets-to-total-liabilities ratio after the deal is _____ times. By paying a premium to Consolidator's tangible asset value, Amalgamator creates $_____ million of goodwill.

Case 4

As the scene opens, an explosive stock market rally has driven up both companies' shares to 3.5 times book value. The ratio of total assets to total liabilities, however, remains at _____ times for Amalgamator and _____ times for Consolidator. As in Case 3, Amalgamator pays a premium of 35.00 percent above the prevailing market price to acquire Consolidator.

	United Amalgamators Corporation	United Consolidators Inc.	Purchase Price	Combined Companies Pro Forma*		
Case 3						
Tangible Assets	1,200	600		1,800		
Intangible Assets (Goodwill)	0	0				
Total Assets	1,200	600		2,067		
Liabilities	800	340		1,140		
					Premium	35%
Shareholders' Equity (SE)	400	260				
Total Liabilities and SE	1,200	600		2,067		
					Multiple	1.5
Total Assets/ Total Liabilities						
Tangible Assets/ Total Liabilities						
Market Capitalization						
Case 4						
Tangible Assets	1,200	600		1,800		
Intangible Assets (Goodwill)	0	0				
Total Assets	1,200	600		2,769		
					Premium	35%
Liabilities	800	340		1,140		
Shareholders' Equity (SE)	400	260				
Total Liabilities and SE	1,200	600		2,769		
					Rally Multiple	3.5
Total Assets/ Total Liabilities						
Tangible Assets/ Total Liabilities						
Market Capitalization						

*Ignores possible impact of EPS dilution.

The premium is calculated on a higher market capitalization, however. Consequently, the purchase price rises from $＿＿＿＿ million to $＿＿＿＿ million. Instead of creating $＿＿＿ million of goodwill, the acquisition gives rise to a $＿＿＿ million intangible asset. Somehow, putting together a company boasting a ＿＿＿＿ times ratio with another sporting a ＿＿＿＿ times ratio has produced an entity with a ratio of ＿＿＿＿ times.

Now, let us exclude goodwill in calculating the ratio of assets to liabilities. Amalgamator's ratio of tangible assets to total liabilities following its acquisition of Consolidator is ＿＿＿＿ times in both Case 3 and Case 4. This is the outcome that best reflects economic reality.

PROJECTING INTEREST EXPENSE

For the following three examples, calculate the embedded cost of Long-Term Debt.

Long-Term Debt (Excluding current maturities)		Colossal Chemical Corporation ($000,000 omitted)	
		2010	2011
Notes Payable Due Dates	Rate		
2012	12.000%	82	44
2013	7.500%	56	80
Debentures Due Dates			
2018	12.500%	55	55
2020	10.875%	120	120
Industrial Development Bonds			
2023	5.875%	40	40
Interest Charges on Long-Term Debt		Average Amount of Total Long-Term Debt Outstanding	Embedded Cost of Long-Term Debt

		Colossal Chemical Corporation ($000,000 omitted)	
Long-Term Debt (Excluding current maturities)		**2010**	**2011**
Notes Payable Due Dates	Rate		
2012	9.500%	96	65
2013	9.750%	65	90
Debentures Due Dates			
2018	11.880%	50	60
2020	12.125%	90	90
Industrial Development Bonds			
2023	5.125%	60	60
Interest Charges on Long-Term Debt		Average Amount of Total Long-Term Debt Outstanding	Embedded Cost of Long-Term Debt

		Colossal Chemical Corporation ($000,000 omitted)	
Long-Term Debt (Excluding current maturities)		**2010**	**2011**
Notes Payable Due Dates	Rate		
2012	6.600%	55	75
2013	5.750%	40	60
Debentures Due Dates			
2018	10.250%	90	90
2020	9.125%	75	75
Industrial Development Bonds			
2023	8.500%	80	80
		340	380
Interest Charges on Long-Term Debt		Average Amount of Total Long-Term Debt Outstanding	Embedded Cost of Long-Term Debt

SENSITIVITY ANALYSIS IN FORECASTING FINANCIAL STATEMENTS

1. Given the base case below, calculate the independent effects of a one percent (1%) increase in Gross Margin, a one percent (1%) decline in the tax rate, and a five percent (5%) increase in Sales.

Colossal Chemical Corporation
Year Ended December 31, 2011
($000,000 omitted)

	Base Case
Sales	$2,110
Cost of goods sold	1,161
Selling, general, and administrative expense	$ 528
Depreciation	121
Research and development	84
Total costs and expenses	1,893
Operating Income	$ 217
Interest expense	34
Interest (income)	(5)
Earnings before Income Taxes	$ 188
Provision for Income Taxes	$ 64
Net Income	$ 124

2. Given the base case below, calculate the independent effects of a two percent (2%) increase in Gross Margin, a two percent (2%) decline in the tax rate, and a five percent (5%) decrease in Sales

Colossal Chemical Corporation
Year Ended December 31, 2011
($000,000 omitted)

	Base Case
Sales	$2,110
Cost of goods sold	1,161
Selling, general, and administrative expense	$ 528
Depreciation	121
Research and development	84
Total costs and expenses	1,893
Operating Income	$ 217
Interest expense	34
Interest (income)	(5)
Earnings before Income Taxes	$ 188
Provision for Income Taxes	$ 64
Net Income	$ 124

3. Given the base case below, calculate the composite effects of a five percent (5%) increase in Sales, a two percent (2%) decline in Gross Margin, a five percent (5%) increase is SG&A as % of Sales, and a two percent (2%) decline in the tax rate.

Colossal Chemical Corporation
Year Ended December 31, 2011
($000,000 omitted)

	Base Case
Sales	$2,110
Cost of goods sold	1,161
Selling, general, and administrative expense	$ 528
Depreciation	121
Research and development	84
Total costs and expenses	1,893
Operating Income	$ 217
Interest expense	34
Interest (income)	(5)
Earnings before Income Taxes	$ 188
Provision for Income Taxes	$ 64
Net Income	$ 124

4. Given the base case below, calculate the independent effects of a one percent (1%) increase in Gross Margin, a one percent (1%) decline in the tax rate, and a five percent (5%) increase in Sales

Impact of Changes in Selected Assumptions on Projected Income Statement

Colossal Chemical Corporation
Year Ended December 31, 2011
($000,000 omitted)

	Base Case
Sales	$2,110
Cost of goods sold	1,477
Selling, general, and administrative expense	$ 253
Depreciation	121
Research and development	84
Total costs and expenses	1,935
Operating Income	$ 175
Interest expense	34
Interest (income)	(5)
Earnings before Income Taxes	$ 146
Provision for Income Taxes	$ 50
Net Income	$ 96

5. Given the base case below, calculate the composite effects of a five percent (5%) increase in Sales, a two percent (2%) decline in Gross Margin, a five percent (5%) increase is SG&A as % of Sales, and a two percent (2%) decline in the tax rate.

Impact of Changes in Selected Assumptions on Projected Income Statement

Colossal Chemical Corporation
Year Ended December 31, 2011
($000,000 omitted)

	Base Case
Sales	$2,110
Cost of goods sold	1,477
Selling, general, and administrative expense	$ 253
Depreciation	121
Research and development	84
Total costs and expenses	1,935
Operating Income	$ 175
Interest expense	34
Interest (income)	(5)
Earnings before Income Taxes	$ 146
Provision for Income Taxes	$ 50
Net Income	$ 96

Two

Answers

Answers to Questions on Each Chapter

CHAPTER 1: THE ADVERSARIAL NATURE OF FINANCIAL REPORTING

1. Three ways that corporations can use financial reporting to enhance their value are:
   a. *Reduce their cost of capital*
   b. *Improve their credit ratings*
   c. *Increase their price-earnings multiple*
2. The true purpose of financial reporting is *to obtain cheap capital.*
3. Corporations routinely *smooth their earnings* because the appearance of *smooth growth* receives a higher *price-earnings* multiple.
4. According to the *"big bath" hypothesis*, reversals of the excess write-offs offer an artificial means of *stabilizing earnings* in subsequent periods.
5. The following are some of the powerful limitations to continued growth faced by companies:
   a. *Entry of competition*
   b. *Increasing base*
   c. *Markets share constraints*
6. Some of the commonly heard rationalizations for declining growth are:
   a. *Our year-over-year comparisons were distorted*
   b. *New products will get growth back on track*
   c. *We're diversifying away from mature markets*
7. *Diversification* reached its zenith of popularity during the *"conglomerate"* movement of the 1960s. However, by the 1980s, the stock market had converted the *diversification premium* into a *conglomerate discount.*
8. *Cross-selling* is one of the ways that the notion of diversification as a means of maintaining *high earnings growth* is revived from time to time.
9. The surprise element in Manville Corporation's 1982 bankruptcy was, in part, a function of *disclosure.*
10. The analysts' heightened awareness of legal risks are a result of bankruptcies associated with:

    a. *Asbestos exposure*
    b. *Silicone gel breast implants*
    c. *Assorted environmental hazards*
11. Some of the stories used to sell stocks to individual investors are:
    a. *A new product with unlimited sales potential*
    b. *A "play" in some current economic trend such as*
      i. *Declining interest rates*
      ii. *Step-up in defense spending*
    c. *Possible corporate takeovers*
12. When the story used to sell stocks to individual investors originates among stockbrokers or even *in the executive offices of the issuer itself,* the zeal with which the story is disseminated may depend more on *its narrative appeal* than the *solidity of the supporting analysis.*
13. The ostensible purpose of financial reporting is *the accurate portrayal* of a corporation's earnings.
14. Over a two-year period BGT paid L&H $35 million to develop translation software. L&H then bought BGT and the translation product along with it. The net effect was that instead *of booking a $35 million research and development expense,* L&H recognized *$35 million of revenue.*

CHAPTER 2: THE BALANCE SHEET

1. A study conducted on behalf of Big Five accounting firm Arthur Andersen showed that between *1978* and *1999,* book value fell from *95* percent to *71* percent of the stock market value of public companies in the United States.
2. As noted by Baruch Lev of New York University, two examples of how traditional accounting systems are at a loss to capture most of what is going on today are:
    a. *The rise in value resulting from a drug passing a key clinical test*
    b. *A computer software program being successfully beta-tested*
3. In the examples in Question 2 there is no accounting event because *no money changes hands.*
4. Some of the distinct approaches that have evolved for assessing real property are:
    a. *Capitalization of rents*
    b. *Inferring a value based on sales of comparable properties*
    c. *Estimating the value a property would have if put to its highest and best use*
5. Some financial assets are unaffected by the difficulties of evaluating physical assets because *they trade daily* in *well-organized markets.*

6. Under the compromise embodied in SFAS 115, financial instruments are valued according to *their intended use* by the *company issuing the financial statements.*

7. If a company wrote off a billion dollars worth of goodwill, its ratio of assets to liabilities would *decline.* Its ratio of *tangible assets to liabilities* would not change, however.

8. Through stock-for-stock acquisitions, the sharp rise in equity prices during the late 1990s was transformed into *increased balance sheet values,* despite the usual assumption that *fluctuations in a company's stock price do not alter its stated net worth.*

9. Unlike *inventories or accounts receivable,* goodwill is not an asset that can be readily *sold or factored* to raise cash. Neither can a company enter into a *sale-leaseback* of its goodwill, as it can with its plant and equipment. In short, goodwill is not *a separable asset* that management can either *convert into cash* or *use to raise cash* to extricate itself from a financial tight spot.

10. A reasonable estimate of a low-profit company's true equity value would be *the amount that produces a return on equity equivalent to the going rate.*

11. Determining the cost of capital is a notoriously controversial subject in the financial field, complicated by *thorny tax considerations* and *risk adjustments.*

12. Among the advantages of market capitalization as a measure of equity are:
    a. *It represents the consensus of investors and analysts who monitor companies' future earnings prospects*
    b. *It can be calculated any day that the stock exchange is open*
    c. *It adjusts instantaneously to news*

13. A limitation of the peer-group approach to valuation is that *it fails to capture company-specific factors* and therefore *does not reap* one major benefit of using *market capitalization* as a gauge of actual equity value.

14. Instead of striving for theoretical purity on the matter, analysts should adopt a *flexible attitude,* using the measure of equity value *most useful to a particular application.*

15. Historical-cost-based balance sheet figures are the ones that matter in *estimating the risk* that a company will violate *a loan covenant* requiring *maintenance of a minimum ratio of debt to net worth.*

16. Users of financial statements can process only *the information they have,* and they do not always have *the information they need.*

17. Deterioration in a company's financial position may catch investors by surprise because it *occurs gradually* and is *reported suddenly.*

CHAPTER 3: THE INCOME STATEMENT

1. Students of financial statements must keep up with *the innovations* of the past few years in transforming *rising stock values* into *revenues of dubious quality.*

2. In the *percentage income statement,* each income statement item is expressed as *a percentage of the "top line"* (sales or revenues), which is represented as *100 percent.*

3. Besides facilitating comparisons between a company's present and past results, the *percentage income statement* can highlight important facts *about a company's competitive standing.*

4. Even within an industry, the breakdown of expenses can vary from company to company as a function of *differing business models* and *financial policies.*

5. Percentage breakdowns are also helpful for comparing a single company's performance with *its results in previous years* and for comparing *two different companies on the basis of their effectiveness in controlling costs.*

6. In essence, Peet's is more of *a coffee roaster* and Starbucks is more involved in *brewing coffee to serve to consumers on premise.*

7. Costs as percentages of sales also vary among companies within an industry for *reasons other* than differences *in business models.*

8. The more widely diversified pharmaceutical manufacturers can be expected to have *higher* percentage *product costs,* as well as *lower* percentage *research and development* expenses, than industry peers that focus exclusively on *prescription drugs.*

9. Analysts must take care not to mistake difference that is actually *a function of business strategy* as evidence of *inferior or superior managerial skills.* A subtler explanation may be available at the modest cost of *contacting some long-established industry watchers.*

10. Executives whose bonuses rise *in tandem with earnings-per-share* have a strong incentive not only *to generate bona fide earnings,* but also to use *every lawful means of inflating the figures through accounting sleight of hand.*

11. On a retrospective basis, a surge *in credit losses* or *an unexpected shortfall in revenues* may indicate that *revenues were inflated in an earlier period.*

12. Along with *employee retirement costs,* another major expense category that can be controlled through *assumptions* is *depreciation.*

13. An unusually low ratio of *depreciation* to *property, plant, and equipment* with the ratios of its industry peers may indicate that management

is being unrealistic in acknowledging the pace of wear and tear on fixed assets. Understatement of *expenses* and overstatement of *earnings* would result.

14. A company knows that creating *more favorable* expectations about *the future* can raise *its stock price* and lower *its borrowing cost.*

15. One way persuading investors that a major development that hurt earnings last year will *not adversely* affect earnings *in future years* is to suggest that any *large loss* suffered by the company was somehow *outside the normal course of business*, and, by implication, *unlikely to recur.*

16. An extraordinary item is reported on an *after-tax* basis, below *the line of income (or loss)* from continuing operations.

17. The accounting rules prohibit corporate officials from displaying certain hits to earnings "above the line," that is, *on a pretax basis*, and from using the label *"extraordinary."* Accordingly they employ designations such as *"nonrecurring"* or *"unusual."* These terms have *no official standing under GAAP*, but *foster the impression that* the highlighted items are *exceptional in nature.*

18. In recent years, *"restructuring"* has become a catchall for charges that companies wish analysts to consider *outside the normal course of business*, but which do not qualify for *below-the-line treatment.*

19. Corporate managers commonly perceive that *the damage to their stock price* will be *no greater* if they take (for sake of argument) a $1.5 billion write-off than if *they write-off $1.0 billion.* The benefit of exaggerating the damage is that in subsequent years, *the overcharges can be reversed in small amounts that do not generate any requirement for specific disclosure.*

20. The most dangerous trap that users of financial statements must avoid walking into, however, is inferring that the term "restructuring" connotes *finality.*

21. The purpose of providing pro forma results was to help analysts *to project future financial results* accurately when some event *outside the ordinary course of business* caused *the unadjusted historical results* to convey a misleading impression.

22. Computer software producers got into the act by *omitting amortization of purchased research and development* from the expenses considered in calculating *pro forma earnings.*

23. Unlike operating income, a concept addressed by FASB standards, *operating earnings* is a number that subjectively *excludes* many *above-the-line "one-time events"* that lack any standing under GAAP.

24. In fact, analysts who hope to forecast future financial results accurately *must* apply *common sense* and set aside genuinely *out-of-the-ordinary-course-of-business events.*

25. Analysts must exercise judgment when considering pro forma earnings; however, they must make sure to examine *the actual SEC filings*, instead of *saving time* by relying solely on *company communications.*

26. An older, but not obsolete, device for beefing up reported income is *capitalization of selected expenditures.*

27. A comparatively *high* ratio of PP&E to *sales* or *cost of goods sold* is another sign of potential trouble.

28. Management can *boost sales* through techniques that more properly fall into the category of *corporate finance.*

29. One way to increase profitability through *external growth* involves *economies of scope.*

30. A corporation can easily accelerate its sales growth by *buying other companies* and *adding their sales to its own.* Creating genuine value for shareholders through *acquisitions* is more difficult, although unwary investors sometimes fail to recognize the distinction.

31. Analysts need to distinguish between *internal growth* and *external growth. Internal growth* consists of sales increases generated from a company's existing operations, while *external growth* represents incremental sales brought in through *acquisitions.*

32. If Company A generates external growth by acquiring Company B and neither Company nor its new subsidiary increases its profitability, then *the intrinsic value of* the merged companies is *no greater* than the sum of the two companies' values.

33. In general, the *less closely related* the combining businesses are, the *less certain* it is that the hoped-for economies of scope *will be realized.*

34. As synergies go, projections of economies of scale in combinations of companies *within the same business* tend to be more plausible than economies of scope purportedly available to companies in *tangentially connected* businesses.

35. A company with relatively large *fixed costs* has a *high* breakeven level. Even a modest economic downturn will reduce *its capacity utilization* below the rate required to keep the company profitable.

36. Deals that work on paper have often foundered on
    a. *incompatible information systems*
    b. *disparate distribution channels*
    c. *clashes of personality among senior executives*
    d. *contrasting corporate culture*

37. Financial statements cannot capture certain *nonquantitative factors* that may be essential to *an evaluation*. These include
   a. *industry conditions*
   b. *corporate culture*
   c. *management's ability to anticipate and respond effectively to change*

CHAPTER 4: THE STATEMENT OF CASH

1. The present version of the statement that traces the flow of funds in and out of the firm, the statement of cash flows, became mandatory, under *SFAS 95*, for issuers with fiscal years ending after *July 15, 1988*.
2. For financial-reporting (as opposed to *tax-accounting*) purposes, a publicly owned company generally seeks to maximize *its reported net income*, which investors use as a basis for valuing its shares.
3. A privately held company, unlike a *public company*, which shows one set of statements to the public and another to the Internal Revenue Service, a private company typically prepares *one set* of statements, with *the tax authorities* foremost in its thinking. Its incentive is not *to maximize*, but to *minimize*, the income it reports, thereby *minimizing* its tax bill as well.
4. In a classic LBO, a group of investors acquires a business by *putting up a small amount of equity* and *borrowing* the balance.
5. The amount attributable to depreciation *does not represent an outlay of cash* in the current year. Rather, it is a bookkeeping entry intended to represent the *gradual reduction in value*, through use, *of physical assets*.
6. Viewed in terms of cash inflows and outflows, rather than earnings, *the leveraged buyout* begins to look like *a sound venture*.
7. Analysts evaluating the investment merits of the LBO proposal would miss the point if they focused on *earnings* rather than *cash flow*.
8. In an LBO, the equity investors do not reap spectacular gains without incurring significant *risk*. There is a danger that everything *will not go according to plan* and that they will lose *their entire investment*. Specifically, there is a risk that *sales and operating earnings* will fall short of expectations, perhaps as a result of *a recession* or because the investors' expectations *were unrealistically high at the outset*.
9. The *cash flow statement*, rather than the *income statement*, provides the best information about a highly leveraged firm's financial health.

10. Among the applications and uses of the Statement of Cash Flows are:
    a. *Determining where a company is in its life cycle*
    b. *Assessing a company's financial flexibility*
    c. *Analyzing a troubled company*
11. When a company is *verging on bankruptcy*, its balance sheet may *overstate its asset value*, as a result of *write-offs* having lagged the *deterioration in profitability* of the company's operations.
12. Revenues build gradually during the *start-up* phase, during which time the company is just *organizing itself* and *launching its products.*
13. Growth and profits accelerate rapidly during the *emerging growth* phase, as the company's products begin to penetrate the market and the *production reaches a profitable scale.*
14. During the *established growth* period, growth in sales and earnings decelerates as the *market nears saturation.* In the *mature industry* phase, sales opportunities are limited to the replacement of products previously sold, plus *new sales derived from growth in the population.*
15. Price competition often intensifies at this stage, as companies *seek sales growth through increased market share.* The *declining industry* stage does not automatically follow maturity, but over long periods some industries do get swept away by *technological change.*
16. Sharply declining sales and earnings, ultimately resulting in *corporate bankruptcies*, characterize industries in decline.
17. *Start-up companies* are typically voracious cash users.
18. *Emerging growth companies* are start-ups that survive long enough to reach the stage of entering the public market.
19. For a company at *the introductory stage*, it may take several years for sales to reach *a level sufficient to cover* sizable fixed costs that are *essential to its operations.*
20. Unlike a *mature company*, Green Mountain is *not self-financing*. It issues substantial *amounts of debt and equity* each year to fund its *growing needs for working capital and acquisitions.*
21. *Established growth companies* are in a less precarious state in terms of cash flow than their emerging growth counterparts.
22. Reflecting the *mature state* of its business, Kimberly-Clark generates a *high and steady* level of *cash from operations.*
23. Far from depending *on external capital*, this mature company *returned capital to investors*, giving them the opportunity to *reinvest* it in higher-growth, *cash-hungry businesses.*
24. Some *mature companies* choose instead to *reinvest their positive cash flow* internally. They either launch or acquire businesses with *higher growth potential than their original, core operations.* The older businesses become *"cash cows" to be milked* for funding the newer activities.

25. *Mature industry companies*, are past the cash strain faced by growth companies that must fund large *construction* programs.

26. *Declining industry companies* struggle to generate sufficient cash as a consequence of meager earnings.

27. By studying the cash flow statement, an analyst can make informed judgments on such questions as:

    a. *How safe (that is, likely to continue being paid) is the company's dividend?*

    b. *Could the company fund its needs internally if external sources of capital suddenly become scarce or prohibitively expensive?*

    c. *Would the company be able to continue meeting its obligations if its business turned down sharply?*

28. In difficult times, when a company must cut back on various expenditures *to conserve cash*, management faces many difficult choices. A key objective is to *avoid damage to the company's long-term health*.

29. At times, *new financing* becomes *painfully expensive*, as a function *of high interest rates* or *depressed stock prices*. During the *"credit crunches"* that occasionally befall the business world, *external financing* is unavailable at any price.

30. If a corporation's financial strain becomes acute, the board of directors may take the comparatively extreme step of *cutting or eliminating the dividend*.

31. Reducing *the dividend* is a step that corporations try very hard to avoid, for fear of *losing favor with investors* and consequently suffering an increase in *cost of capital*.

32. A final factor in assessing financial flexibility is the change in adjusted working capital. Unlike conventional working capital *(current assets minus current liabilities)*, this figure excludes *notes payable*, as well as *cash* and *short-term investments*.

33. A company with a strong balance sheet can fund much of that cash need by increasing its *trade payables* (credit extended by vendors). External financing may be needed, however, if accumulation of unsold goods causes *inventories* to rise disproportionately to *sales*. Similarly, if customers begin paying more slowly than formerly, *receivables* can widen the gap between *working capital requirements* and *trade credit availability*.

34. One typical consequence of violating *debt covenants* or striving to head off *bankruptcy* is that management reduces discretionary expenditures to avoid *losing control*.

35. Overinvestment has unquestionably led, in many industries, to prolonged periods of *excess capacity*, producing in turn chronically *poor profitability*. In retrospect, the firms involved would have served their

shareholders better if they had *increased their dividend payouts* or *repurchased stock*, instead of *constructing new plants*.

36. Keeping cash "trapped" in marketable securities can enable a firm *to gain an edge* over "lean-and-mean" competitors when *tight credit conditions* make it difficult to *finance working capital needs*.

37. Another less obvious risk of eschewing financial flexibility is the danger of permanently losing *experienced skilled workers* through *temporary layoffs* occasioned by recessions.

38. The income statement is a dubious measure of the success of a *highly leveraged* company that is being managed to *minimize*, rather than *maximize*, reported profits.

39. The cash flow statement is the best tool for measuring *flexibility*, which, contrary to a widely held view, is not merely a security blanket for *squeamish investors*.

40. In the hands of an aggressive but prudent management, a cash flow cushion can enable a company to *sustain essential long-term investment spending* when competitors are forced to cut back.

CHAPTER 5: WHAT IS PROFIT?

1. Profitability is a yardstick by which businesspeople can measure their *achievements* and justify *their claims to compensation*.

2. When calculating *bona fide* profits, the analyst must take care to consider only genuine revenues and deduct all relevant costs.

3. There can be no bona fide profit without *an increase in wealth*. Bona fide profits are the only kind of profits *that truly matter* in financial analysis.

4. Merely *circulating funds*, it is clear, does not increase wealth.

5. An essential element of genuinely useful financial statement analysis is *the willingness to take accounting profits at something other than face value*.

6. The issuer of the statements can *raise* or *lower* its reported earnings simply by using its latitude to assume shorter or longer *average lives for its depreciable assets*.

7. The rate at which the tax code allows owners to write-off property overstates *actual wear-and-tear*.

8. In the *broadcasting business*, companies typically record depreciation and amortization expense that far exceeds physical wear-and-tear on assets.

9. In many industries, fixed assets consist mainly of *machines or vehicles that really do diminish in value through use*. The major risk of

analytical error does not arise from the possibility that *reported depreciation expense will substantially exceed economic depreciation*, but the reverse.

CHAPTER 6: REVENUE RECOGNITION

1. Many corporations employ **highly aggressive recognition** practices that comply with GAAP yet **distort the underlying economic reality.**
2. Under intense pressure to maintain their stock prices, companies characterized by *extremely rapid sales growth* seem particularly prone *to take liberties.*
3. To seasoned investors, *an abrupt departure* by a senior manager represents *a telltale sign of trouble.*
4. Bonus-seeking managers may initially veer off the straight-and-narrow by *"borrowing"* a small amount from *future revenue*, intending to *"pay it back"* the following year, but they instead fall further and further behind. Eventually, the gap between *reported revenues* and *economic reality* grows too large to sustain.
5. Even when an independent accounting firm certifies that a company's financials *have been prepared in accordance* with generally accepted accounting principles; the analyst must stay alert for evidence *that the numbers misrepresent the economic reality.*
6. Staying alert to evidence of flawed, *or possibly fraudulent*, reporting is essential, even when the auditors *put their blessing on the numbers.*
7. As a rule, distorting one section of the financial statements *throws the numbers out of whack in some other section.* Assiduous tracking of a variety of *financial ratios* should raise serious questions about a company's reporting, at a minimum.
8. The explanation for the sudden drop in projected earnings was that in 2001 Bristol-Myers *gave wholesalers discounts* to induce them *to buy its products* at a much faster rate than necessary *to fill prescriptions at pharmacies.*
9. *"Channel-stuffing"* is a security analysts' term for the financial reporting gimmick that Bristol-Myers employed *to accelerate future revenues to the current period.*
10. Along with other pharmaceutical producers, Bristol-Myers was feeling profit pressures due to *difficulties in developing new drugs* to replace sales of products *on which patent protection was expiring.*
11. Haydon was known for speaking candidly about Bristol-Myers's declining sales prospects. Consequently, his reassignment was *taken as a message that executives must meet their sales quotas at all costs.*

12. Also suspect was Bristol-Myers's repeated practice of *establishing restructuring reserves* that exactly equaled *gains on asset sales*.

13. The Bristol-Myers Squibb case study nevertheless illustrates the value of *testing a company's reported earnings* against *independently provided information*.

14. According to Take-Two management, the adjustment arose because the company *recorded revenue* on some games it sold to *"certain independent third-party distributors"* but which were later *returned to or repurchased* by Take-Two.

15. *Contrary* to the lesson taught by many other cases of financial misreporting, it paid to accept the Take-Two *discredited management's* assurances that the company's business prospects *looked bright*.

16. Take-Two shipped hundreds of thousands of video games to distributors *who were under no obligation to pay for them, fraudulently* booked the shipments *as if they were sales*, then *accepted returns of the products* in later periods.

17. Encouragingly for users of financial statements, managers *who improperly recognize revenues* are often betrayed by *the number trails they create*.

18. In layaway sales, customers reserve goods *with down payments*, and then make additional payments over a specified period, *receiving their merchandise* when they have paid in full.

19. Prior to the change in accounting practice, which FAS 101 made mandatory, Wal-Mart booked layaway sales *as soon as it placed the merchandise on layaway*. Under the new and more conservative method, the company began to recognize the sales *only when customers completed the required payments and took possession of the goods*.

20. On the whole, Bally's reported profit margins benefited from the increase in *financed memberships* as a percentage of total revenues. The reported earnings, however, rested on assumptions regarding the percentage of customers who *would ultimately fail to make all of the scheduled installments*.

21. As in any sales situation, aggressive pursuit of new business could result in *acceptance of more marginally qualified customers*. On average, the newer members might prove to be *less financially capable* or less committed to physical fitness than *the previous purchasers of financed memberships*.

22. There was no change in the accounting principle, namely, *the matching concept*. In the case of a health club, members' upfront fees represent *payments for services received over the terms of their membership*. Club operators should therefore recognize the revenue over the period in which *they render the service*.

23. Under GAAP, the general requirement was to spread membership fees *over the full membership period*. If a company offered refunds, it could not *book any of the revenue* until the refund period expired, unless there was *a sufficiently long history* to enable management to estimate *future experience* with reasonable confidence.

24. Under certain circumstances, a company engaged in long-term contract work can *book revenue before billing its customer*. This result arises from GAAP's solution to a mismatch commonly observed *at construction firms*.

25. GAAP addresses the problem through the **percentage-of-completion method**, which permits the company to recognize revenue in *proportion to the amount of work completed*, rather than in line with its billing.

26. As is generally the case with *artificial acceleration*, taking liberties with the percentage-of-completion borrows *future revenues*, making a surprise *shortfall inevitable* at some point.

27. The SEC claimed that management at Sequoia Systems inflated revenue and profits by:
    a. *Booking letters of intent as revenue*
    b. *Backdating some purchase orders*
    c. *Granting customers special terms that Sequoia never disclosed*

28. The SEC also claimed that management at Sequoia Systems profited from the scheme by *selling stock before a true picture of the company's financial condition emerged*.

29. Loading the distribution channels consists of *inducing distributors or retailers* to accept larger shipments of goods than *their near-term sales expectations warrant*.

30. Loading does not boost *physical sales volume*, but merely shifts the timing of its *recognition as reported revenues*.

31. Inevitably, the underlying trend of final sales to consumers slows down, at least temporarily. At that point, the manufacturer's growth in reported revenue will maintain its trend only *if its distributors take on even bigger inventories*, relative to their sales. If the distributors balk, *the loading scheme will unravel*, forcing a *sizable write-off* of previously recorded profits.

32. Krispy Kreme revised its senior executive compensation plan.[1] Henceforth, officers would receive *no bonuses* unless the company *reported earnings* in each quarter *that exceeded its earnings per share* guidance *by at least $0.01*.

---

[1]*SEC v. Scott A. Livengood, John W. Tate, and Randy S. Casstevens; SEC Complaint against Scott A. Livengood, John W. Tate, and Randy S. Casstevens*, May 4, 2009.

33. In essence, according to the *Wall Street Journal*'s story, Krispy Kreme *manufactured earnings* by taking money *out of one pocket and putting it into another.*

34. Had Krispy Kreme instead *repurchased the franchises and then closed the stores*, it would have *incurred an expense.* The catch is that an asset is supposed to be *something that creates future economic value.* Terminated stores would not seem *to satisfy that definition.*

35. Most, if not all, of the *cash* on Krispy Kreme's *balance sheet* appeared to have come from a *sale-and-leaseback* transaction, rather than from *operations.*

36. Krispy Kreme increased the size of the corrections to its fiscal 2004 results. The previously undisclosed problems involved *derivatives transactions, errors in accounting for leases and improvements related to leases,* and *reversal of income related to equipment sold to a franchisee before Krispy Kreme bought that operation.*

37. Krispy Kreme was *not a case of massively* fictitious earnings. Rather, the SEC complaint depicted *a process of nickel-and-diming*, through a wide range of *financial statement items*, to beat *earnings guidance by $0.01 in every single quarter.*

38. An exceptionally long record of *beating guidance* or *posting year-over-year gains in quarterly earnings* is a reason to *suspect earnings management.*

39. A second lesson of the Krispy Kreme case is that *related-party transactions* and *deceptive financial reporting* often go hand in hand.

40. It is impossible to assess the quality of an internal investigation without information on the *methods employed* and the basis *for its conclusions.*

41. Users of financial statements should not be intimidated by corporate *press releases* that denounce allegedly irresponsible *securities analysts and journalists.*

42. In 2001, Halliburton adopted an even more aggressive approach to *recognizing revenue.* For some projects, Halliburton began reporting sales *months before billing customers for the work.* Previously, the policy was to book revenues *only if the company expected to bill clients within one month.* In addition, the company began keeping some disputed bills on the books *for over a year instead of writing them off and reporting losses.* The previous policy was to refrain from a write-off only *if it believed it would collect most of the claim within one year.*

43. Halliburton became more aggressive about *booking revenues before getting paid*, a classic technique for *pumping up reported earnings.*

44. If earnings look suspiciously *strong* during a *rough patch* for the company's industry, users of financial statements should *never automatically rule out the possibility that manipulative accounting* explains the disparity.

45. A stock's value is a function of expected *future earnings,* which partly depend on the *popularity of the company's products* vis-à-vis its competitors'.

46. Generally, the initial response of corporate executives caught in a lie is *to dig themselves a deeper hole,* but gratifyingly often, *the truth ultimately emerges.*

47. Analysts who strive to go beyond routine *number-crunching* can profit by seeking *independent verification* of corporate disclosure, even when *the auditors* have already placed *their stamp of approval on it.*

48. Sometimes, management *delays* revenue recognition in order to *understate* short-run profits. The motive for this paradoxical behavior is a desire to report the sort of *smooth year-to-year earnings growth* that equity investors reward with *high price-earnings multiples.*

49. Grace executives reckoned that with earnings already meeting Wall Street analysts' forecasts, a windfall *would not help* the company's stock price. Such an inference would have been consistent with investors' customary *downplaying of profits and losses* that they perceive to be generated by *one-time events.*

50. Grace's 1998 statement that its auditors had raised no objections to its accounting for the Medicare reimbursement windfall was true only *in the technical sense* that Price Waterhouse issued clean financials, based on materiality considerations. As a spokeswoman for the auditing firm pointed out, such an opinion *does not imply agreement with everything in the statements.*

51. According to Michael Jensen: "Tell a manager that he will get a bonus when targets are realized and two things will happen":
    a. *Managers will attempt to set easy targets.*
    b. *Once these are set, they will do their best to see that they are met even if it damages the company.*

52. All too often, companies wouldn't be able to accomplish the frauds without *the assistance of their customers.*

53. According to Jensen, almost every company uses a budget system that *rewards* employees for *lying* and punishes them *for telling the truth.* He proposes reforming the system by severing the link between *budget targets* and *compensation.*

54. Even in the case of the bluest of the blue chips, watching for rising levels of *accounts receivable* or *inventory,* relative to *sales,* should be standard operating procedure.

55. When the revenues derived from *wishful thinking* fail to materialize, the managers may resort to *fraud to maintain the illusion*. The positive mental attitude that overstates revenues in the early stage *is no less damaging*, however, than *the fraud responsible* at a later point.

CHAPTER 7: EXPENSE RECOGNITION

1. Corporate managers are just as creative *in minimizing* and *slowing down* the recognition of *expenses* as they are in maximizing and speeding up the *recognition of revenues*.
2. Investors attach little significance to *nonrecurring* profits and losses in valuing stocks. Therefore, a public company has a strong incentive to *aggregate cumulative losses* into a one-time event and to *break up a unique*, nonrecurring *gain* into smaller pieces and *recognize it over several years*.
3. Nortel Networks illustrated *the distorting power of accruals*, one of the most *abused features* of financial reporting.
4. Between September 2000 and *August 2002*, Nortel's market capitalization sank *by 99 percent*, devastating *Canadian pension plans* that were heavily invested in its shares.
5. The company had to wave a *classic red flag* with respect to *the credibility of its financial statements* by *delaying the filing of its 2003* financial reports.
6. In addition to dashing hopes *that the new round of accounting statements would be minor*, Nortel rattled the market by *firing CEO Dunn, CFO Beatty, and controller Gollogly*.
7. Nortel's management's credibility *continued to shrink* as the *company kept pushing back its target date* for producing definitive *earnings restatements*.
8. Nortel's investigation, which previously had focused on *accruals and provisions*, had turned to *revenue recognition*.
9. Incorrect recognition of that amount resulted from a combination of:
   a. *Non-transfer of legal title to customers*
   b. *Failure to meet criteria for recognizing revenue prior to shipment*
   c. *The collectibility questions*
   d. *Other incorrect steps*
10. Nortel followed a strategy of *taking a "big bath"* in its money-losing period of 2001–2002. *Overstating losses* created *"cookie cutter" reserves* that could be taken *into profits in later years*.
11. Nortel's experience shows that if a company *uses accruals to understate profits*, it will have no compunction about *overstating profits* through *aggressive revenue recognition*.

12. An important takeaway from the Nortel case is that *seemingly small items* can prove *highly significant.*
13. *Rebates* are another frequently abused element of *expense recognition.* General Motors's fiddling with this device *shows the important role of corporate culture* in the *integrity* of financial reporting.
14. At issue in GM's restatement was *the recording of rebates* and *other credits* from *suppliers.*
15. GM said that some cash flows from *its mortgage subsidiary* that should have been classified among its *investing activities* were instead booked as *operating activities.*
16. This revelation puzzled accounting experts because the applicable rules were unambiguous. *Extending a loan* or *receiving repayment* fell into *investing activities; interest payments* were included in *operating cash flow.*
17. GM Management said it had *prematurely increased the value of vehicles* it was leasing to car-rental companies, assuming they would be *worth* more after those companies *were through with them.*
18. Ordinarily, a company's stock price *rises* when its reported earnings *unexpectedly increase.*
19. Freddie Mac steadfastly *denied* that its handling of *derivatives* was aimed at *smoothing its earnings.*
20. Even if it was true that *intentional misrepresentations* represented the *lesser part of the earnings understatement,* Freddie Mac's *questionable practices* had a huge impact that even *conscientious analysts* could not detect *from the outside.*
21. Freddie Mac's manipulation did not end there. Another ploy to *hide earnings* consisted of ceasing to use *market prices for certain derivatives.*
22. Companies can follow a variety of approaches in downplaying expenses such as:
    a. *Making liberal assumptions about costs that may be capitalized*
    b. *Diluting expenses with one-time gains*
    c. *Jumping the gun in booking rebates from suppliers*
    d. *Understating expenses through sheer sloppiness in their bookkeeping*

CHAPTER 8: THE APPLICATIONS AND LIMITATIONS OF EBITDA

1. The impetus for trying to redirect investors' focus to *operating income* or other variants has been *the minimal net profits* recorded by many "new economy" companies.

2. Users of financial statements had discovered certain limitations in net income as a *valuation tool*. They observed that two companies in the same industry could report similar *income*, yet have substantially different *total enterprise values*.

3. Net income is not, to the disappointment of analysts, a standard by which every company's *value* can be compared.

4. The accounting standards leave companies considerable discretion regarding the *depreciable lives* they assign to their *property, plant, and equipment*. The same applies to amortization schedules for *intangible assets*.

5. For some companies, the sum of net income, income taxes, and interest expense is not equivalent to EBIT, reflecting the presence of such factors as *extraordinary items and minority interest* below *the pretax income line*.

6. Shifting investors' attention away from traditional fixed-charge coverage and toward *EBITDA coverage of interest* was particularly beneficial during the 1980s, when some buyouts were so *highly leveraged* that *projected EBIT* would not cover pro forma interest expense even in a good year.

7. Capital spending is likely to exceed depreciation over time as the company *expands its productive capacity* to accommodate *rising demand*. Another reason that capital spending may run higher than depreciation is that newly acquired equipment may be *costlier* than the old equipment being written off, as a function of *inflation*.

8. Delaying equipment purchases and repairs that are needed but not *urgent*, should inflict no lasting damage on the company's *operations* provided the *profit slump* lasts for only a few quarters.

9. Depreciation is not available as a long-run source of cash for *interest payments*. This was a lesson applicable not only to extremely *leveraged* deals of the 1980s, but also to the more *conservatively* capitalized transactions of later years.

10. Beaver's definition of cash flow was more stringent than *EBITDA* since he did not add back either *taxes* or *interest* to net income.

11. Beaver did not conclude that analysts should rely solely on the *cash-flow-to-debt ratio*, but merely that it was the single best *bankruptcy predictor*.

12. Some investment managers consider that the single ratio of *cash flow* (as they define it) to *fixed charges* predicts bankruptcy better than all of *the rating agencies'* quantitative and qualitative considerations combined.

13. Aside from *seasonal variations*, the amount of working capital needed to run a business represents a fairly constant *percentage* of a company's

sales. Therefore, if inventories or receivables *increase* materially as a percentage of sales, analysts should strongly suspect that the earnings are *overstated*, even though management will invariably offer a *more benign* explanation.

14. If a company resorts to stretching out its payables, two other ratios that will send out warning signals are:

   a. *Receivables to sales*

   b. *Inventories to cost of goods sold*

15. Merrill Lynch investment strategist Richard Bernstein points out that *operating* earnings tend to be more stable than *reported* earnings, EBIT tends to be more stable than *operating* earnings, and *EBITDA* tends to be more stable than EBIT.

16. Strategist Bernstein found that by attempting to *filter out the volatility* inherent in companies' earnings, investors reduced the *effectiveness* of their stock selection.

CHAPTER 9: THE RELIABILITY OF DISCLOSURE AND AUDITS

1. Fear of the consequences of breaking the law keeps corporate managers in line. <u>Bending</u> the law is another matter, though, in the minds of many executives. If their bonuses depend on *presenting results in an unfairly favorable light*, they can usually see their way clear to adopting that course.

2. Technically, *the board of directors* appoints the auditing firm, but *management* is the point of contact in hashing out the details of presenting financial events for *external consumption*.

3. At some point, *resigning the account* becomes a moral imperative, but in the real world, accounting firms must be *pushed rather far to reach that point*.

4. It is common for front-line auditors to balk at an *aggressive accounting treatment* proposed by a company's managers, only to be overruled by *their senior colleagues*.

5. *Fraud* is an unambiguous violation of accounting standards, but audits do not *invariably catch it*.

6. Extremely clever scamsters may even succeed in undermining the auditors' efforts to select *their samples at random*, a procedure designed to foil concealment of fraud.

7. When challenged on inconsistencies in their numbers, companies sometimes *blame error*, rather than any intention to *mislead the users of financial statements*.

8. Seasoned followers of the corporate scene realize that companies are not always as *forthcoming* as investors *might reasonably expect.*
9. According to president and chief executive of Trump World's Fair Casino Hotel, the firm's focus in 1999 was threefold:
   a. *To increase our operating margins at each operating entity*
   b. *To decrease our marketing costs*
   c. *To increase our cash sales from our non-casino operations*
10. Investors who relied solely on *the disclosure* by Trump World's Fair Casino Hotel were burned if they bought into the rally that followed the *bullish-sounding* press release.
11. Abundant evidence has emerged over the years of corporate managers *leaning on auditors* to paint as rosy a picture as possible.
12. To say that *no perfect system can be designed,* however, is quite different from saying that
   a. *Existing provisions for issuing financial accounting standards*
   b. *Conducting audits*
   c. *Policing fraud are as good as real-world conditions permit*
13. Popular outrage over the *post–Tech Wreck* accounting scandals created *political momentum* to eliminate *the auditing-consulting conflict.*
14. Systematic problems in the audit process arise not only *from the regulatory structure* but also from *the business strategies* of *profit-maximizing accounting firms.*
15. In the 1990s, *"risk-based audits"* emerged as a means of keeping a lid on costs. Instead of focusing on *details of individual transactions,* they identified the areas that in *their judgment* presented the greatest risk of error or fraud, such as *complex derivatives.* Incredibly, these judgments in some cases were based on *management's advice.*
16. In WorldCom's early days, Arthur Andersen audited the company in *a meticulous, bottom-up way.* As the company grew, however, Andersen migrated toward *a risk-based process.* If a question arose about controls or procedures, Andersen relied on the *answers provided by management.*
17. Congress's unwillingness to give the SEC *the resources it needed to do its job* reflected more than *competing claims* on *the federal budget.*
18. One final line of defense for users of a company's financial statements is *the audit committee of its board of directors.* This protection has *not proven infallible* over the years.
19. In one of the few encouraging notes of recent years, the SEC has imposed a *"financial literacy"* requirement on audit committee members.
20. Many companies are either *stingy with information* or *slippery about the way they present it.* Rather than laying down the law (or GAAP), the auditors typically wind up *negotiating with management* to arrive

at a point where they can convince themselves that *the bare minimum requirements of good practice* have been satisfied.

21. Given the observed gap between *theory* and *practice* in financial reporting, users of financial statements must provide themselves *an additional layer of protection* through tough *scrutiny of the numbers.*

CHAPTER 10: MERGERS-AND-ACQUISITIONS ACCOUNTING

1. Choosing a method of accounting for a merger or acquisition does not affect the combined companies' subsequent *competitive strength* or *ability to generate cash.* The discretionary accounting choices can have a *substantial impact,* however, on *reported earnings.*

2. Meyer emphasized that he was *not accusing* Tyco *of fraud,* but merely of *aggressive accounting.* Nevertheless, the diversified manufacturer responded in the *classic of manner of a company criticized for tricky financial reporting;* Tyco angrily denounced Meyer's report, stating that *"rumors relating to the company are false, unfounded, and malicious."*

3. Alert analysts had suspected something was going on behind the scenes. They questioned why in the most recent fiscal year, *debt attributable* to Tyco's *industrial businesses* doubled to $21.6 billion even though the company reported $4.8 billion *in free cash flow.*

4. Swartz acknowledged that the amount spent on *unannounced deals* was not determinable from Tyco's financial statements because it reported *acquisition expenditures net of cash on the acquired companies' balance sheets* and did not disclose the *aggregate amount of that cash.*

5. The investigators concluded that Tyco repeatedly used aggressive, *albeit legal, accounting gimmicks,* including *depressing the reported profits of acquired companies* immediately before acquisition, in order to generate *profit surges in the first quarter after closing.* Company officials referred to such practices as *"financial engineering"* and ordered employees to "create stories" to justify *accounting changes that would hype Tyco's reported earnings.*

6. Tyco's financial reporting aggressiveness involved *distortion of reported free cash flow* through a nonstandard definition of the term. Tyco excluded *cash received from sales of receivables* and *cash outlays for the purchase of customer accounts* for its ADT security-alarm business, labeling the latter *"acquisitions."*

7. Although the pooling-of-interests method has been abolished, M&A accounting remains an area in which analysts must be on their toes.

Companies have developed *increasingly subtle strategies* for exploiting the discretion afforded by the rules. *Maximizing reported earnings* in the post-acquisition period remains a key objective.

8. For example, one M&A-related gambit entails the GAAP-sanctioned use, for financial reporting purposes, of *an acquisition date other than the actual date on which a transaction is consummated.* Typically, companies use this discretion to simplify the closing of their books at month- or quarter-end.

9. Under Securities and Exchange Commission rules, companies do not have to *restate previous statements* to reflect the revenues and earnings of acquired businesses *deemed immaterial in size.*

10. There can be no guarantee of loans secured by stock issued in the combination, which would effectively *negate the transfer of risk* implicit in a bona fide *exchange of securities. Reacquisitions* of stock, and *special distributions* are likewise prohibited.

11. Regulators may tighten up rules that can be abused, such as the *standards for materiality*, but corporate managers usually manage to stay one step ahead. Analysts who hope to keep pace would do well to study *the classic gambits employed in the M&A area,* in order to understand the thought process of the field's most notorious innovators.

12. Clues to hanky-panky may include:
    a. *An unusually large number of special items*
    b. *A mysterious buildup of cash despite large reported free cash flow*
        If an acquired company was a public reporter prior to its acquisition
    c. *A drop in earnings just prior to closing*

CHAPTER 11: IS FRAUD DETECTABLE?

1. Beneish defines manipulation to include both *actual fraud* and *the management of earnings or disclosure within GAAP.*

2. Beneish finds, by statistical analysis, that the presence of any of the following five factors increases the probability of earnings manipulation:
   1. *Increasing days sales in receivables*
   2. *Deteriorating gross margins*
   3. *Decreasing rates of depreciation*
   4. *Decreasing asset quality (defined as the ratio of noncurrent assets other than property, plant, and equipment to total assets)*
   5. *Growing sales*

3. The evidence of criminal misrepresentation *often appears obvious after the fact,* but *not even the most skilled analysts* definitively identified

some of the most famous frauds *until the schemes became unsustainable* and the companies *collapsed.*

4. In studying these notorious frauds, readers should pay close attention *not only to the suspicious financial statement items,* but also *to the behavior of senior managers* as the validity of their stated profits is challenged.

5. Unexpected *turnover in senior management* is a classic warning sign of financial misrepresentation.

6. When Enron at long last conceded that it was overly indebted, management tried to:
   a. *Restructure existing debt*
   b. *Arrange additional borrowings*
   c. *Obtain equity infusions*
   d. *Raise cash by selling overseas assets*

7. Enron also misled investors by aggressively exploiting wiggle room in the accounting rules. The company booked revenue from its energy-related derivatives contracts on the basis of *gross value,* rather than *net value,* as is the norm for *other securities transactions.*

8. Excessive liberties with *mark-to-market* accounting rules constituted yet one more element of Enron's misrepresentation.

9. On a conference call dealing with Enron's earnings, analyst Richard Grubman complained that the company was *unique* in refusing to include a *balance sheet* in its earnings release.

10. Still, the *off-balance-sheet* vehicles, combined with *non-transparent disclosures,* enabled Enron to make itself look less *debt-laden* than it really was.

11. While Enron grossly misled investors by *stretching the rules,* a large part of its deception consisted of *outright violation of* basic accounting standards, with *the acquiescence* of its auditor.

12. Equally crude was a scheme in which Enron reportedly borrowed $500 million from a bank and *bought Treasury bills.* A few days later it sold the *Treasury bills* and repaid the bank, reporting the proceeds from the meaningless transaction as *operating cash flow.*

13. The *opacity* of Enron's *fair value assumptions* was a major concern. "Ultimately they're telling you *what they think the answer is,* but they're not telling you *how they got to that answer,*" Business Valuation Services analyst Stephen Campbell complained. "That is essentially saying '*trust me.*'"

14. Off Wall Street consulting group recommended a short sale of Enron based on two factors identifiable from the financial statements, namely, *the mark-to-market on non-traded assets* and *related-party transactions* with *private partnerships.*

15. Analysts should be especially wary when *a strong likelihood of financial manipulation*, as indicated by tools such as *the Beneish model*, coincides with *non-transparent* financial reporting.

16. According to the SEC's complaint, HealthSouth's falsification began *shortly after the company went public in 1986.*

17. Flat denial by Scrushy, regardless *of the evidence that emerged*, was a consistent theme as the *HealthSouth story* unfolded.

18. The complaint stated that when HealthSouth officials and accountants urged Scrushy *to cease inflating profits*, he replied, in effect, "*not until I sell my stock.*"

19. The "Sarbox" provision requiring CFOs and CEOs to attest to the accuracy of financial statements gave prosecutors a powerful weapon to wield against falsifiers, but *HealthSouth's fraud* dispelled any notion that the tough new law *would end financial misreporting altogether.*

20. HealthSouth exaggerated its earnings by understating the gap between *the cost of a treatment* and *the amount that the patient's insurance would cover.*

21. If the auditors did question an accounting entry, HealthSouth executives reportedly *created a phony document* to validate the item.

22. HealthSouth also propped up profits by *failing to write-off receivables* with *little chance of being collected.* In addition, the company *did not recognize losses* when it sold assets *that had declined in value.*

23. Compounding Scushy's legal problems, federal prosecutors disclosed in July 2003 that they had uncovered evidence of:
    a. *Tax fraud*
    b. *Obstruction of justice*
    c. *Witness intimidation*
    d. *Money laundering*
    e. *Public corruption*

24. The most dismaying aspect of the performance of HealthSouth's auditor, Ernst & Young LLP, was *its failure* to challenge a *sudden, large increase* in cash.

25. In the view of experts in the field, internal checks and balances also broke down at HealthSouth. The board's audit committee met *only once* during 2001, *three times less* than the minimum recommended by the SEC.

26. Investors had little official warning of trouble until *the month before* Parmalat's collapse. As late as October 2003, Deutsche Bank's equity research group rated the company's stock *a BUY*, highlighting *its strong reported cash flow*, and Citibank put out *an optimistic* report in November. Furthermore, the company's debt carried

an *investment grade* rating up until *nine days before* the bankruptcy filing.

27. A major red flag was Parmalat's *voracious appetite for debt*, despite claiming to have a *huge cash balance*.

28. Merrill Lynch analysts downgraded Parmalat to SELL, saying that the company's *frequent recourse to the bond market*, while reporting *high cash balances*, threw into question *its cash-generating ability*.

29. Another hazard signal emerged on February 26, 2003, when Parmalat suddenly canceled its plan *to sell 30-year bonds*. The company said it would instead *issue bonds with maturities of just seven years*, suggesting the market had less confidence in Parmalat's *long-run stability* than management had thought.

30. Oddly, the person who achieved the greatest renown for early recognition of the Parmalat's house of cards was not *a financial analyst*, but a *comedian*.

CHAPTER 12: FORECASTING
FINANCIAL STATEMENTS

1. It is *future earnings and dividends* that determine the value of a company's stock and the *relative likelihood of future timely payments of debt service* that determines credit quality.

2. The process of financial projections is an extension of *historical patterns* and *relationships*, based on assumptions about future *economic conditions, market behavior*, and *managerial action*.

3. Sales projections for the company's business can be developed with the help of such sources as *trade publications, trade associations*, and firms that sell *econometric forecasting* models.

4. Basic industries such as *chemicals, paper*, and *capital goods* tend to lend themselves best to the *macroeconomic-based approach* described here. In technology-driven industries and "hits-driven" businesses such as *motion pictures* and *toys*, the connection between *sales* and the *general economic trend* will tend to be looser.

5. The expected intensity of industry competition, which affects a company's *ability to pass cost increases* on to customers or to retain *cost decreases*, influences the *gross margin* forecast.

6. Since the segment information in may show only operating income, and not *gross margin*, the analyst must add *segment depreciation* to operating income, then make assumptions about the allocation of *selling, general*, and *administrative expense* and *research and development* expense by segment.

7. The R&D percentage may change if, for example, the company *makes a sizable acquisition* in an industry that is either significantly more, or significantly less, *research-intensive* than its existing operations.

8. The key to the forecasting interest expense method employed here is to estimate the firm's embedded cost of debt, that is, the *weighted average interest rate* on the company's *existing long-term debt.*

9. Accurately projecting interest expense for *highly leveraged* companies is important because *their financial viability* may depend on the size of *the interest expense "nut"* they must cover each quarter.

10. The completed income statement projection supplies *the first two lines* of the projected statement of cash flows.

11. Before assuming a constant-percentage relationship, the analyst must verify that *the most recent year's ratios are representative of experience over several years.*

12. A sizable *net cash provision* might be presumed to be directed toward share repurchase, reducing *shareholders' equity,* if management has indicated a desire to *buy stock* and is *authorized to do so* by its board of directors.

13. Typically, the analyst must modify the underlying *economic* assumptions, and therefore the projections, several times during the year as *business activity* diverges from *forecasted levels.*

14. A firm may have considerable room to cut *its capital spending* in the short run if it suffers a decline in funds provided by *operations.* A projection that ignored this *financial flexibility* could prove overly pessimistic.

15. An interest rate decline will have limited impact on a company for which interest costs represent a *small percentage of expenses.* The impact will be greater on a company with a large interest cost component and with much of its debt at *floating rates.* This assumes the return on the company's assets is *not similarly rate-sensitive.*

16. Analysts are generally not arrogant enough to try to forecast the figures accurately to the first decimal place, that is, to the *hundred-thousands* for a company with revenues in the *hundreds of millions.*

17. It is generally inappropriate to compare a *quarterly income statement* item (EBITDA) with a balance sheet figure, especially in the case of a *highly seasonal* company.

18. It is unwise to base an investment decision on historical statements that antedate a major financial change such as:
    a. *Stock repurchase*
    b. *Write-off*
    c. *Acquisition*
    d. *Divestment*

19. A pro forma income statement for a single year provides no information about *the historical growth* in sales and earnings of *the subsidiary* that is being spun off.

20. Pro forma adjustments for a divestment do not capture the potential benefits of increased *management focus* on the company's *core operations.*

21. The earnings shown in a merger-related pro forma income statement may be higher than the company can sustain because:
    a. The acquired company's owners may be shrewdly selling out at top dollar, anticipating a *deceleration in earnings growth* that is foreseeable by *industry insiders*, but not to the acquiring corporation's management.
    b. Mergers of companies in the same industry often work out poorly due to *clashes of corporate culture.*
    c. Inappropriately applying *its management style* to an industry with very different requirements.

22. A *fixed-income* investor buying a 30-year bond is certainly interested in the issuer's financial prospects beyond *a 12-month horizon.* Similarly, a substantial percentage of the present value of future dividends represented by a stock's price lies *in years beyond the coming one.*

23. Radical financial restructurings such as *leveraged buyouts, megamergers massive stock*, and *buybacks* necessitate *multiyear* projections.

24. Of the various types of analysis of financial statements, projecting *future results* and *ratios* requires the greatest skill and produces *the most valuable findings.*

25. The lack of *predictable patterns* is what makes financial forecasting so *valuable.* When betting huge sums in the face of *massive uncertainty*, it is essential that investors understand *the odds* as fully as they possibly can.

CHAPTER 13: CREDIT ANALYSIS

1. Financial statements tell much about a borrower's *ability* to repay a loan, but disclose little about the equally important *willingness* to repay.

2. If a company is dependent on raw materials provided by a subsidiary, there may be a *reasonable* presumption that it will stand behind the subsidiary's *debt*, even *in the absence of a formal guarantee.*

3. Illiquidity manifests itself as an excess of current *cash payments due*, over *cash currently available.* The *current* ratio gauges the risk of this

occurring by comparing the claims against the company that will become payable during *the current operating cycle (current liabilities)* with the assets that are already in the form of cash or that will be converted to cash during *the current operating cycle (current assets)*.

4. The greater the amount by which asset values could deteriorate, the greater the *"equity cushion,"* and the greater the creditor's sense of *being protected*. Equity is by definition *total assets* minus *total liabilities*.

5. Aggressive *borrowers* frequently try to satisfy the letter of a *maximum* leverage limit imposed by lenders, without fulfilling the *conservative spirit* behind it.

6. A firm that "zeros out" its *short-term debt* at some point in each operating cycle can legitimately argue that its "true" leverage is represented by the *permanent (long-term) debt* on its balance sheet.

7. Current maturities of long-term debt should enter into the calculation of *total debt*, based on a conservative assumption that the company will replace maturing debt with *new long-term borrowings*.

8. Exposure to interest rate fluctuations can also arise from long-term *floating-rate debt*. Companies can limit this risk by using *financial derivatives*.

9. Public financial statements typically provide *only general* information about the extent to which the issuer has *limited* its exposure to interest rate fluctuations through *derivatives*.

10. Analysts should remember that the ultimate objective is not to *calculate ratios* but to *assess credit risk*.

11. In general, the credit analyst must recognize the heightened level of risk implied by the presence of preferred stock in the *capital structure*. One formal way to take this risk into account is to calculate the ratio of *total fixed obligations* to *total capital*.

12. In addition to including capital leases in the total debt calculation, analysts should also take into account the *off-balance-sheet* liabilities represented by contractual payments on *operating leases*, which are reported as *rental expense* in the *Notes* to Financial Statements.

13. A corporation can employ leverage yet avoid showing debt on its consolidated balance sheet by *entering joint ventures* or forming *partially owned subsidiaries*.

14. Under SFAS 87, balance sheet recognition is now given to pension liabilities related to employees' service to date. Similarly, SFAS 87 requires recognition of postretirement health care benefits as an on-balance sheet liability.

15. The precise formula for *calculating* a ratio is less important than the assurance that it is *calculated consistently* for all companies being evaluated.

16. In general, credit analysts should assume that the achievement of *higher* bond ratings is a *secondary* goal of corporate management.

17. The contemporary view is that profits are ultimately what sustain *liquidity* and *asset values*. High profits keep plenty of cash flowing through the system and confirm the value of productive assets such as *plant* and *equipment*.

18. The cumulative effect of a change in accounting procedures will appear *"below the line,"* or after *income taxes* have already been deducted. The sum of net income and provision for income taxes will then differ from the *pretax income figure* that appears in the income statement.

19. Operating margin shows how well management has run the business *buying and selling* wisely, controlling *selling and administrative expenses* before taking into account financial policies, which largely determine *interest expense*, and *the tax rate*, which is outside management's control.

20. Fixed-charge coverage is an *income-statement* ratio of major interest to credit analysts. It measures the ability of a company's *earnings* to meet the *interest payments* on its debt, the lender's most direct concern. In its simplest form, the fixed-charge coverage ratio indicates the *multiple* by which *operating earnings* suffice to pay *interest charges*.

21. Regardless of whether it is *expensed* or *capitalized*, however, all interest accrued must be covered by *earnings* and should therefore appear in the *denominator* of the fixed-charge coverage calculation.

22. The two complications that arise in connection with incorporating operating lease payments into the fixed-charge coverage calculation are:
    a. *The SEC does not require companies to report rental expense in quarterly statements*
    b. *Retailers in particular often negotiate leases with rents that are semifixed, tied in part to revenues of the leased stores*

23. Companies sometimes argue that the denominator of the fixed-charge coverage ratio should include only *net interest* expense, that is, the difference between *interest expense* and income derived from *interest-bearing assets*, generally consisting of marketable securities.

24. Ratios related to sources and uses of funds measure credit quality at the most elemental level—a company's ability to *generate sufficient cash to pay its bills*.

25. Given corporations' general reluctance to sell new equity, a recurrent cash shortfall is likely to be made up with *debt* financing, leading to a rise in *the total-debt-to-total-capital* ratio.

26. A company that suffers a prolonged downtrend in its ratio of *cash flow to capital expenditures* is likely to get more deeply into debt, and therefore become *financially riskier* with each succeeding year.

27. Unlike earnings, *depreciation* is essentially a programmed item, a cash flow assured by the accounting rules. The higher the percentage of cash flow derived from *depreciation*, the higher is the *predictability* of a company's cash flow, and the *less dependent* its financial flexibility on the vagaries of the marketplace.

28. Analysts cannot necessarily assume that all is well simply because capital expenditures consistently exceed depreciation. Among the issues to consider are:

   a. *Persistent inflation means that a nominal dollar spent on plant and equipment today will not buy as much capacity as it did when the depreciating asset was acquired*

   b. *Technological advances in production processes may mean that the cost in real terms of producing one unit may have declined since the company purchased the equipment now being replaced*

   c. *Depreciation may be understated, with respect either to wear-and-tear or to obsolescence*

   d. *In a growth industry, a company that fails to expand its capacity at roughly the same rate as its competitors may lose essential economies of scale and fall victim to a shakeout*

29. A limitation of combination ratios that incorporate balance-sheet figures is that they have little meaning if *calculated for portions of years.*

30. The underlying notion of a turnover ratio is that a company requires a certain level of *receivables* and *inventory* to support a given volume of sales.

31. A *drop in sales* is a possible explanation of declining inventory turnover. In this case, the inventory may not have suffered a severe reduction in value, but there are nevertheless unfavorable implications for *credit quality*. Until the inventory glut can be worked off by *cutting back production* to match the lower *sales volume*, the company may have to borrow to finance its unusually high working capital, thereby increasing its *financial leverage*.

32. Fixed-charge coverage, too, has a weakness, for it is based on *earnings*, which are subject to considerable manipulation.

33. Built from two comparatively hard numbers, the ratio of *total debt* to *cash flow* provides one of the best single measures of *credit quality*.

34. Expected *recoveries* have an important bearing on the decision to *extend* or *deny* credit, as well as on the *valuation* of debt securities.

35. Line of business is another basis for defining *a peer group.*

36. Beyond a certain point, calculating and comparing companies on the basis of *additional* financial ratios contributes little *incremental insight*.

37. *Improving* or *deteriorating* financial ratios can have different implications for different companies.
38. Quantitative models such as Zeta, as well as others that have been devised using various mathematical techniques, have several distinct benefits such as:
    a. *They are developed by objectively correlating financial variables with defaults*
    b. *The record of quantitative models is excellent from the standpoint of classifying as troubled credits most companies that subsequently defaulted*
    c. *The scores assigned to nondefaulted companies by these models correlate fairly well with bond ratings*
39. Like the quantitative models consisting of *financial ratios,* the default risk models based on stock prices provide useful, but *not infallible,* signals.

CHAPTER 14: EQUITY ANALYSIS

1. In this chapter, the discussion focuses primarily on the use of financial statements in *fundamental analysis.*
2. Of the methods of fundamental common stock analysis, no other approach matches the intuitive appeal of regarding the stock price as the *discounted value* of expected *future* dividends. This approach is analogous to the *yield-to-maturity* calculation for a bond and therefore facilitates the comparison of different *securities* of a single *issuer.*
3. By thinking through the logic of the *discounting* method, the analyst will find that value always comes back to *dividends.*
4. The company's earnings growth rate may diverge from its sales growth due to changes in its *operating margins.*
5. As a rule, a *cyclical* company will not increase its dividend on a regular, annual basis.
6. Many analysts argue that *cash flow,* rather than *earnings,* is the true determinant of dividend-paying capability.
7. Cash generated from *operations,* which is generally more difficult for companies to manipulate than *earnings,* can legitimately be viewed as the preferred measure of future *dividend-paying capability.*
8. The ability to vary the *discount rate,* and therefore to assign a *lower* or *higher* multiple to a company's earnings, is the equity analyst's defense against earnings *manipulation* by management.

9. It is appropriate to assign an *above-average* discount factor to the earnings of a company that competes against larger, better-capitalized firms. A small company *may also suffer the disadvantages of lack* of depth in management and concentration of *its production in one or two plants.*

10. A building-materials manufacturer may claim to be cushioned against fluctuations in housing starts because of a strong emphasis in its product line on *the remodeling and repair markets.*

11. Analysts should be especially wary of companies that have tended to jump on the bandwagon of *"concepts"* associated with the *hot stocks* of the moment.

12. Earnings per share will not grow merely because *sales increase.*

13. Leverage reaches a limit, since lenders will not continue advancing funds beyond a certain point as *financial risk increases.*

14. One way to increase earnings per share is to *reduce the number of shares outstanding.*

15. To the extent that the company funds share buybacks with idle cash, the increase in *earnings per share* is offset by a reduction arising from *forgone income on investments.*

16. Like most ratio analysis, the Du Pont Formula is valuable not only for *the questions it answers* but also for *the new ones it raises.*

17. Besides introducing greater volatility into the *rate of return,* adding debt to the balance sheet demonstrates *no management skill in improving operations.*

18. Some companies have the potential to raise their share prices by *utilizing their assets more efficiently,* while others can increase their value by *increasing their financial leverage.*

19. Management's main adversaries in battles over *"corporate governance"* were aggressive *financial operators.*

20. At least in the early stages, before some raiders became overly aggressive in their financial forecast assumptions, it was feasible to extract value without creating undue bankruptcy risk, simply by *increasing the ratio of debt to equity.*

21. In future bear markets, when stocks again sell at depressed price-earnings multiples, investors will probably renew their focus on *companies' values as LBO candidates.*

22. A leveraged buyout can bring about improved profitability for either of two reasons:
    a. *A change in ownership results in a fresh look at the company's operations*
    b. *Management may obtain a significantly enlarged stake in the firm's success as the result of the buyout*

23. Today's *profit improvement* may be a precursor of tomorrow's bankruptcy by a company that has economized its way to *an uncompetitive state.*

24. A focus on *price-earnings* multiples, the best-known form of fundamental analysis, is not the investor's *sole alternative* to relying on technicians' stock charts.

25. For the investor who takes a longer view, *financial statement analysis* provides an invaluable reference point for valuation.

Financial Statement Exercises

1. Indicate in which of the principal financial statements each item appears.
   a.

Item	Balance Sheet	Income Statement	Statement of Cash Flows
Accounts Payable	×		
Accumulated Depreciation	×		
Adjusted Net Income		×	
Capital Expenditures			×
Cash and Equivalents—Change		×	
Common Shares Outstanding	×		
Current Debt—Changes		×	
Direct Operating Activities			×
Earnings per Share (Fully Diluted)		×	
Earnings per Share (Primary)		×	
Equity in Net Loss (Earnings)			×
Extraordinary Items		×	
Financing Activities—Net Cash Flow			×
Gross Plant, Property, and Equipment	×		
Income before Extraordinary Items		×	×
Indirect Operating Activities			×
Interest Paid—Net			×
Investing Activities			×
Investment Tax Credit	×		
Long-Term Debt Due in One Year	×		
Minority Interest	×	×	
Net Receivables	×		
Operating Activities—Net Cash Flow			×
Other Assets and Liabilities—Net Change			×
Other Investments	×		
Preferred Stock—Nonredeemable	×		
Pretax Income		×	
Retained Earnings	×		
Sale of Property, Plant, and Equipment			×

(*Continued*)

Item	Balance Sheet	Income Statement	Statement of Cash Flows
Selling, General, and Administrative Expense		×	
Stock Equivalents		×	
Total Current Assets	×		
Total Income Taxes		×	
Total Preferred Stock	×		

b.

Item	Balance Sheet	Income Statement	Statement of Cash Flows
Accrued Expenses	×		
Adjusted Available for Common		×	
Available for Common		×	
Cash and Equivalents	×		
Common Equity	×		
Cost of Goods Sold		×	
Deferred Taxes	×		×
Dividends per Share		×	
Earnings per Share (Primary)		×	
Equity	×		
Financing Activities			×
Funds from Operations—Other			×
Income Taxes Paid			×
Interest Expense		×	
Inventory—Decrease (Increase)			×
Investing Activities—Other			×
Investments at Equity	×		
Long-Term Debt	×		
Long-Term Debt—Reduction			×
Net Plant, Property, and Equipment	×		
Notes Payable	×		
Other Assets	×		
Other Current Liabilities	×		
Preferred Dividends		×	
Prepaid Expenses	×		
Receivables—Decrease (Increase)			×
Sale of Investments			×
Savings Due to Common		×	
Special Items		×	
Total Assets	×		
Total Equity	×		
Total Liabilities and Equity	×		

c.

Item	Balance Sheet	Income Statement	Statement of Cash Flows
Accounts Payable and Accrued Liabilities—Increase (Decrease)			×
Acquisitions			×
Assets	×		
Capital Surplus	×		
Cash Dividends			×
Common Stock	×		
Deferred Charges	×		
Discontinued Operations		×	
Earnings per Share (Fully Diluted)		×	
EPS from Operations		×	
Exchange Rate Effect			×
Financing Activities—Other			×
Gross Profit		×	
Income Taxes—Accrued—Increase (Decrease)			×
Intangibles	×		
Inventories	×		
Investing Activities—Net Cash Flow			×
Investments—Increase			×
Liabilities	×		
Long-Term Debt—Issuance			×
Minority Interest		×	
Non-Operating Income/Expense		×	
Operating Profit		×	
Other Current Assets	×		
Other Liabilities	×		
Preferred Stock—Redeemable	×		
Purchase of Common and Preferred Stock			×
Sale of Common and Preferred Stock			×
Sales		×	
Short-Term Investments—Change			×
Taxes Payable	×		
Total Current Liabilities	×		
Total Liabilities	×		
Treasury Stock	×		

2. The common size form of the Balance Sheet

Cracker Barrel Old Country Store, Inc. (NasdaqGS:CBRL)
In Millions of USD, except per share items.

	Balance Sheet					
Balance Sheet as of:	Reclassified Jul-28-2006	Aug-03-2007	Aug-01-2008	Jul-31-2009	Jul-30-2010	5-Yr Avg.
ASSETS						
Cash and Equivalents	5.22%	1.13%	0.91%	0.93%	3.69%	
Total Cash & ST Investments	5.22%	1.13%	0.91%	0.93%	3.69%	
Accounts Receivable	0.68%	0.93%	1.03%	1.02%	1.05%	
Other Receivables	0.00%	0.00%	0.53%	0.33%	0.00%	
Total Receivables	0.68%	0.93%	1.55%	1.35%	1.05%	
Inventory	7.63%	11.42%	11.87%	11.04%	11.15%	
Prepaid Exp.	0.26%	1.00%	0.84%	0.74%	0.67%	
Deferred Tax Assets, Curr.	1.04%	0.99%	1.38%	1.87%	1.73%	
Other Current Assets	24.05%	0.37%	0.25%	0.00%	0.00%	
Total Current Assets	38.89%	15.83%	16.80%	15.93%	18.29%	
Gross Property, Plant & Equipment	84.18%	118.59%	119.65%	126.28%	125.50%	
Accumulated Depreciation	(25.75)%	(38.04)%	(40.09)%	(45.83)%	(47.78)%	
Net Property, Plant & Equipment	58.44%	80.55%	79.56%	80.45%	77.71%	75%
Other Long-Term Assets	2.67%	3.62%	3.64%	3.62%	4.00%	
Total Assets	100.00%	100.00%	100.00%	100.00%	100.00%	
LIABILITIES						
Accounts Payable	4.22%	7.36%	7.09%	7.40%	8.99%	
Accrued Exp.	8.30%	10.61%	8.44%	8.90%	9.16%	
Curr. Port. of LT Debt	0.48%	0.65%	0.66%	0.59%	0.52%	
Curr. Port. of Cap. Leases	0.00%	0.00%	0.00%	0.00%	0.00%	
Curr. Income Taxes Payable	1.27%	1.43%	0.00%	0.00%	0.59%	
Unearned Revenue, Current	1.12%	1.67%	1.72%	1.81%	2.13%	
Other Current Liabilities	4.26%	0.00%	2.24%	2.58%	2.55%	
Total Current Liabilities	19.66%	21.71%	20.15%	21.28%	23.96%	

Balance Sheet						
Balance Sheet as of:	Reclassified Jul-28-2006	Aug-03-2007	Aug-01-2008	Jul-31-2009	Jul-30-2010	5-Yr Avg.
Long-Term Debt	54.21%	59.79%	62.32%	56.16%	49.53%	
Capital Leases	0.00%	0.00%	0.01%	0.00%	0.00%	
Pension & Other Post-Retire. Benefits	0.00%	0.00%	0.00%	0.00%	2.01%	
Def. Tax Liability, Non-Curr.	4.87%	4.94%	4.14%	4.47%	4.42%	
Other Non-Current Liabilities	3.28%	5.34%	6.33%	7.20%	5.25%	
Total Liabilities	82.02%	91.77%	92.94%	89.11%	85.17%	
Common Stock	0.02%	0.02%	0.02%	0.02%	0.02%	
Additional Paid in Capital	0.25%	0.00%	0.06%	1.04%	0.48%	
Retained Earnings	17.98%	8.92%	9.09%	13.43%	18.11%	
Treasury Stock	0.00%	0.00%	0.00%	0.00%	0.00%	
Comprehensive Inc. and Other	(0.27)%	(0.71)%	(2.11)%	(3.60)%	(3.78)%	
Total Common Equity	17.98%	8.23%	7.06%	10.89%	14.83%	
Total Equity	17.98%	8.23%	7.06%	10.89%	14.83%	
Total Liabilities and Equity	100.00%	100.00%	100.00%	100.00%	100.00%	
Supplemental Items						
Total Shares Out. on Balance Sheet Date	1.84%	1.87%	1.70%	1.82%	1.76%	
Total Debt	54.69%	60.43%	62.99%	56.76%	50.06%	
Net Debt	49.47%	59.31%	62.08%	55.83%	46.37%	
Debt Equivalent Oper. Leases	25.86%	35.11%	35.24%	38.81%	40.78%	35%
Finished Goods Inventory	6.80%	8.69%	10.81%	10.05%	10.16%	
Other Inventory Accounts	0.84%	2.73%	1.06%	0.98%	0.99%	
Land	16.51%	22.76%	22.81%	22.98%	22.26%	
Buildings	57.55%	54.31%	54.12%	55.15%	54.05%	
Machinery	0.00%	26.63%	27.33%	30.47%	31.76%	
Construction in Progress	1.07%	1.56%	1.15%	1.29%	0.89%	
Leasehold Improvements	8.87%	13.08%	13.99%	16.12%	16.28%	14%
Assets under Cap. Lease, Gross	0.20%	0.26%	0.25%	0.26%	0.25%	

Chipotle Mexican Grill, Inc. (NYSE:CMG)
In Millions of USD, except per share items.

Balance Sheet						
Balance Sheet as of:	Dec-31-2005	Dec-31-2006	Dec-31-2007	Dec-31-2008	Dec-31-2009	5-Yr Avg.
ASSETS						
Cash and Equivalents	0.02%	25.43%	20.94%	10.67%	22.84%	
Short-Term Investments	0.00%	0.00%	2.77%	12.12%	5.20%	
Total Cash & ST Investments	0.02%	25.43%	23.70%	22.79%	28.04%	
Accounts Receivable	0.49%	0.81%	0.74%	0.44%	0.50%	
Other Receivables	0.57%	1.45%	1.32%	0.03%	0.00%	
Total Receivables	1.07%	2.26%	2.06%	0.48%	0.50%	
Inventory	0.67%	0.58%	0.60%	0.58%	0.58%	
Prepaid Exp.	2.19%	1.18%	1.25%	1.43%	1.50%	
Deferred Tax Assets, Curr.	0.60%	0.15%	0.34%	0.31%	0.33%	
Other Current Assets	0.00%	0.00%	0.00%	0.00%	0.00%	
Total Current Assets	4.54%	29.60%	27.95%	25.58%	30.94%	
Gross Property, Plant & Equipment	108.82%	86.46%	89.45%	94.23%	91.74%	
Accumulated Depreciation	(22.01)%	(19.46)%	(20.91)%	(23.21)%	(25.55)%	
Net Property, Plant & Equipment	**86.80%**	**66.99%**	**68.54%**	**71.02%**	**66.19%**	72%
Goodwill	4.52%	2.94%	3.04%	2.66%	2.28%	
Deferred Tax Assets, LT	3.46%	0.00%	0.00%	0.00%	0.00%	
Other Long-Term Assets	0.68%	0.48%	0.47%	0.74%	0.59%	
Total Assets	100.00%	100.00%	100.00%	100.00%	100.00%	
LIABILITIES						
Accounts Payable	3.36%	3.24%	2.75%	2.90%	2.62%	
Accrued Exp.	5.91%	5.47%	6.14%	5.43%	6.59%	
Curr. Port. of LT Debt	0.01%	0.01%	0.01%	0.01%	0.01%	
Curr. Income Taxes Payable	0.00%	0.25%	0.00%	0.00%	0.44%	
Unearned Revenue, Current	0.95%	1.16%	1.25%	0.97%	0.97%	
Other Current Liabilities	0.46%	0.00%	0.00%	0.00%	0.00%	
Total Current Liabilities	10.70%	10.13%	10.15%	9.31%	10.62%	
Long-Term Debt	0.89%	0.67%	0.55%	0.47%	0.39%	
Def. Tax Liability, Non-Curr.	0.00%	3.09%	2.28%	3.62%	4.04%	
Other Non-Current Liabilities	9.60%	7.67%	9.18%	11.14%	11.78%	
Total Liabilities	21.18%	21.56%	22.16%	24.53%	26.84%	

Balance Sheet						
Balance Sheet as of:	Dec-31-2005	Dec-31-2006	Dec-31-2007	Dec-31-2008	Dec-31-2009	5-Yr Avg.
Common Stock	0.07%	0.05%	0.05%	0.04%	0.03%	
Additional Paid in Capital	95.73%	77.90%	67.76%	60.85%	56.15%	
Retained Earnings	(9.81)%	0.49%	10.04%	18.27%	28.86%	
Treasury Stock	0.00%	0.00%	0.00%	(3.66)%	(11.89)%	
Comprehensive Inc. and Other	(7.18)%	0.00%	0.00%	(0.02)%	0.00%	
Total Common Equity	78.82%	78.44%	77.84%	75.47%	73.16%	
Total Equity	78.82%	78.44%	77.84%	75.47%	73.16%	
Total Liabilities and Equity	100.00%	100.00%	100.00%	100.00%	100.00%	
Supplemental Items						
Total Shares Out. on Balance Sheet Date	6.70%	5.39%	4.54%	3.90%	3.27%	
Total Debt	0.90%	0.68%	0.56%	0.48%	0.40%	
Net Debt	0.88%	(24.74)%	(23.14)%	(22.32)%	(27.63)%	
Debt Equivalent Oper. Leases	83.30%	64.18%	77.59%	88.19%	84.28%	80%
Land	1.67%	1.36%	1.14%	1.00%	0.93%	
Buildings	81.77%	0.00%	0.00%	0.00%	0.00%	
Machinery	25.38%	19.89%	20.49%	21.80%	21.53%	
Leasehold Improvements	81.77%	65.21%	67.82%	71.43%	69.29%	71%
Employees	3,312.14%	2,482.59%	2,603.46%	2,472.77%	2,314.08%	

Buffalo Wild Wings Inc. (NasdaqGS:BWLD)
In Millions of USD, except per share items.

Balance Sheet						
Balance Sheet as of:	Dec-25-2005	Dec-31-2006	Dec-30-2007	Reclassified Dec-28-2008	Dec-27-2009	5-Yr Avg.
ASSETS						
Cash and Equivalents	2.99%	7.29%	0.77%	3.42%	3.10%	
Short-Term Investments	36.37%	32.78%	33.75%	14.83%	14.12%	
Total Cash & ST Investments	39.37%	40.07%	34.52%	18.25%	17.22%	

(Continued)

Balance Sheet						
Balance Sheet as of:	Dec-25-2005	Dec-31-2006	Dec-30-2007	Reclassified Dec-28-2008	Dec-27-2009	5-Yr Avg.
Accounts Receivable	0.55%	0.58%	0.45%	0.37%	0.69%	
Other Receivables	2.78%	3.23%	4.50%	3.02%	2.99%	
Total Receivables	3.33%	3.81%	4.95%	3.39%	3.68%	
Inventory	1.13%	1.10%	1.20%	1.27%	1.18%	
Prepaid Exp.	1.48%	0.65%	1.55%	1.35%	0.96%	
Deferred Tax Assets, Curr.	0.58%	0.87%	0.66%	0.71%	0.95%	
Other Current Assets	0.00%	0.00%	0.00%	3.15%	7.89%	
Total Current Assets	45.88%	46.50%	42.88%	28.12%	31.88%	
Gross Property, Plant & Equipment	83.21%	82.41%	86.11%	96.63%	96.44%	
Accumulated Depreciation	(31.62)%	(33.94)%	(33.99)%	(33.30)%	(35.07)%	
Net Property, Plant & Equipment	51.60%	48.48%	52.13%	63.34%	61.36%	55%
Goodwill	0.28%	0.23%	0.19%	4.50%	3.64%	
Other Intangibles	0.21%	0.23%	0.21%	3.00%	2.16%	
Other Long-Term Assets	2.03%	4.56%	4.60%	1.04%	0.97%	
Total Assets	100.00%	100.00%	100.00%	100.00%	100.00%	
LIABILITIES						
Accounts Payable	4.98%	3.64%	5.42%	6.85%	4.35%	
Accrued Exp.	8.02%	10.24%	9.55%	7.61%	8.44%	
Curr. Income Taxes Payable	0.08%	0.16%	0.00%	0.00%	0.00%	
Unearned Revenue, Current	1.65%	1.46%	1.18%	1.03%	0.88%	
Other Current Liabilities	0.45%	0.49%	0.33%	4.28%	7.92%	
Total Current Liabilities	15.18%	15.99%	16.48%	19.77%	21.58%	
Def. Tax Liability, Non-Curr.	3.57%	1.96%	1.10%	3.66%	4.83%	
Other Non-Current Liabilities	8.50%	9.94%	10.54%	6.20%	5.69%	
Total Liabilities	27.25%	27.90%	28.12%	29.62%	32.11%	

				Balance Sheet		
Balance Sheet as of:	Dec-25-2005	Dec-31-2006	Dec-30-2007	Reclassified Dec-28-2008	Dec-27-2009	5-Yr Avg.
Common Stock	55.97%	46.55%	41.01%	35.40%	30.38%	
Additional Paid in Capital	0.00%	0.00%	0.00%	0.00%	0.00%	
Retained Earnings	18.71%	25.55%	30.87%	34.97%	37.51%	
Treasury Stock	0.00%	0.00%	0.00%	0.00%	0.00%	
Comprehensive Inc. and Other	(1.95)%	0.00%	0.00%	0.00%	0.00%	
Total Common Equity	72.75%	72.10%	71.88%	70.38%	67.89%	
		0.00%				
Total Equity	72.75%	72.10%	71.88%	70.38%	67.89%	
Total Liabilities and Equity	100.00%	100.00%	100.00%	100.00%	100.00%	
Supplemental Items						
Net Debt	(39.36)%	(40.08)%	(34.50)%	(18.25)%	(17.21)%	
Debt Equivalent Oper. Leases	72.65%	75.00%	70.37%	73.43%	72.21%	73%
Buildings	48.48%		0.81%	2.72%	5.93%	
Machinery	34.01%	33.50%	35.50%	39.15%	39.20%	
Construction in Progress	0.72%	0.64%	0.94%	4.39%	2.08%	
Leasehold Improvements	48.48%	48.26%	48.87%	50.36%	49.21%	49%

Denny's Corporation (NasdaqCM:DENN)
In Millions of USD, except per share items.

			Balance Sheet			
Balance Sheet as of:	Restated Dec-28-2005	Restated Dec-27-2006	Restated Dec-26-2007	Restated Dec-31-2008	Dec-30-2009	5-Yr Avg.
ASSETS						
Cash and Equivalents	5.52%	5.90%	5.71%	6.16%	8.48%	
Total Cash & ST Investments	5.52%	5.90%	5.71%	6.16%	8.48%	

(Continued)

			Balance Sheet			
Balance Sheet as of:	Restated Dec-28-2005	Restated Dec-27-2006	Restated Dec-26-2007	Restated Dec-31-2008	Dec-30-2009	5-Yr Avg.
Accounts Receivable	3.29%	3.38%	3.60%	4.43%	5.79%	
Notes Receivable	0.00%	0.00%	0.00%	0.00%	0.00%	
Total Receivables	3.29%	3.38%	3.60%	4.43%	5.79%	
Inventory	1.61%	1.85%	1.72%	1.60%	1.33%	
Prepaid Exp.	1.64%	2.04%	2.52%	2.79%	3.05%	
Other Current Assets	0.00%	1.07%	1.78%	0.67%	0.00%	
Total Current Assets	12.06%	14.23%	15.34%	15.64%	18.66%	
Gross Property, Plant & Equipment	131.03%	138.52%	130.29%	130.17%	124.81%	
Accumulated Depreciation	(74.66)%	(85.36)%	(81.36)%	(83.35)%	(82.75)%	
Net Property, Plant & Equipment	**56.36%**	**53.17%**	**48.92%**	**46.80%**	**42.06%**	**49%**
Goodwill	9.82%	11.27%	11.25%	10.13%	10.38%	
Other Intangibles	14.02%	16.56%	18.27%	18.83%	19.04%	
Loans Receivable Long-Term	0.00%	0.00%	0.00%	0.00%	0.00%	
Deferred Charges, LT	3.08%	1.42%	1.35%	1.13%	0.86%	
Other Long-Term Assets	4.67%	3.35%	4.88%	7.46%	9.01%	
Total Assets	100.00%	100.00%	100.00%	100.00%	100.00%	
LIABILITIES						
Accounts Payable	9.31%	9.49%	11.46%	7.39%	7.31%	
Accrued Exp.	13.81%	11.81%	15.58%	15.33%	14.05%	
Curr. Port. of LT Debt	0.37%	1.24%	0.55%	0.41%	0.29%	
Curr. Port. of Cap. Leases	1.22%	1.57%	1.07%	1.03%	1.19%	
Curr. Income Taxes Payable	0.00%	2.65%	2.57%	2.59%	2.54%	
Other Current Liabilities	4.32%	3.80%	3.60%	4.59%	4.08%	
Total Current Liabilities	29.03%	30.56%	34.84%	31.34%	29.46%	
Long-Term Debt	101.08%	93.57%	86.38%	87.95%	82.81%	
Capital Leases	**5.65%**	**5.61%**	**5.52%**	**6.46%**	**6.30%**	**6%**
Pension & Other Post-Retire. Benefits	0.00%	0.00%	0.97%	4.44%	3.17%	

	Balance Sheet					
Balance Sheet as of:	Restated Dec-28-2005	Restated Dec-27-2006	Restated Dec-26-2007	Restated Dec-31-2008	Dec-30-2009	5-Yr Avg.
Def. Tax Liability, Non-Curr.	0.00%	2.73%	3.07%	3.61%	4.16%	
Other Non-Current Liabilities	16.38%	17.84%	17.51%	18.69%	14.88%	
Total Liabilities	152.13%	150.32%	148.29%	152.50%	140.78%	
Common Stock	0.18%	0.21%	0.25%	0.28%	0.31%	
Additional Paid in Capital	101.29%	118.80%	141.41%	157.67%	173.55%	
Retained Earnings	(149.79)%	(165.41)%	(186.46)%	(203.16)%	(208.81)%	
Treasury Stock	0.00%	0.00%	0.00%	0.00%	0.00%	
Comprehensive Inc. and Other	(3.81)%	(3.92)%	(3.47)%	(7.29)%	(5.82)%	
Total Common Equity	(52.13)%	(50.32)%	(48.28)%	(52.49)%	(40.78)%	
Total Equity	(52.13)%	(50.32)%	(48.28)%	(52.49)%	(40.78)%	
Total Liabilities and Equity	100.00%	100.00%	100.00%	100.00%	100.00%	
Supplemental Items						
Total Debt	108.31%	102.00%	93.53%	95.86%	90.59%	
Net Debt	102.79%	96.10%	87.82%	89.70%	82.11%	
Debt Equivalent Oper. Leases	**80.15%**	**91.20%**	**106.04%**	**116.53%**	**124.88%**	**104%**
Finished Goods Inventory	0.00%	0.00%	1.72%	1.60%	1.33%	
Land	11.12%	8.44%	7.62%	6.93%	5.76%	
Buildings	**92.88%**	**88.48%**	**74.04%**	**71.15%**	**66.86%**	**79%**
Machinery	27.02%	0.00%	0.00%	0.00%	0.00%	
Assets under Cap. Lease, Gross	7.35%	8.90%	5.47%	5.66%	3.94%	
Assets under Cap. Lease, Accum. Depr.	(3.33)%	(4.55)%	(3.23)%	(3.07)%	(1.89)%	
Assets on Oper. Lease, Gross	0.00%	0.00%	12.74%	16.54%	19.52%	
Assets on Oper. Lease, Accum. Depr.	0.00%	0.00%	(9.30)%	(10.83)%	(12.79)%	

California Pizza Kitchen Inc. (NasdaqGS:CPKI)
In Millions of USD, except per share items.

			Balance Sheet			
Balance Sheet as of:	Jan-01-2006	Reclassified Dec-31-2006	Reclassified Dec-30-2007	Dec-28-2008	Jan-30-2010	5-Yr Avg.
ASSETS						
Cash and Equivalents	4.11%	2.64%	2.94%	3.91%	6.12%	
Short-Term Investments	4.16%	0.00%	0.00%	0.00%	0.00%	
Total Cash & ST Investments	8.27%	2.64%	2.94%	3.91%	6.12%	
Accounts Receivable	1.50%	2.54%	0.56%	0.75%	0.92%	
Other Receivables	0.00%	0.00%	2.81%	1.93%	2.66%	
Total Receivables	1.50%	2.54%	3.36%	2.68%	3.58%	
Inventory	1.38%	1.53%	1.41%	1.47%	1.59%	
Prepaid Exp.	2.00%	1.74%	1.59%	0.51%	2.00%	
Deferred Tax Assets, Curr.	3.08%	3.77%	1.91%	1.63%	2.02%	
Other Current Assets	0.52%	0.00%	0.00%	0.00%	0.00%	
Total Current Assets	16.74%	12.21%	11.22%	10.19%	15.30%	
Gross Property, Plant & Equipment	145.58%	150.69%	148.05%	160.42%	172.14%	
Accumulated Depreciation	(67.78)%	(68.44)%	(66.92)%	(80.21)%	(99.21)%	
Net Property, Plant & Equipment	**77.81%**	**82.25%**	**81.13%**	**80.21%**	**72.92%**	79%
Goodwill	0.00%	0.00%	0.00%	1.25%	1.32%	
Other Intangibles	2.18%	2.50%	2.39%	1.32%	1.35%	
Deferred Tax Assets, LT	1.65%	1.89%	3.75%	5.62%	7.14%	
Other Long-Term Assets	1.62%	1.16%	1.51%	1.41%	1.97%	
Total Assets	100.00%	100.00%	100.00%	100.00%	100.00%	
LIABILITIES						
Accounts Payable	2.57%	4.84%	5.46%	3.35%	3.22%	
Accrued Exp.	12.99%	13.80%	13.52%	13.45%	15.25%	
Curr. Port. of LT Debt	0.00%	0.00%	5.72%	0.00%	0.00%	
Curr. Income Taxes Payable	0.00%	1.16%	0.26%	1.12%	0.00%	

		Balance Sheet				
Balance Sheet as of:	Jan-01-2006	Reclassified Dec-31-2006	Reclassified Dec-30-2007	Dec-28-2008	Jan-30-2010	5-Yr Avg.
Unearned Revenue, Current	0.00%	0.00%	2.18%	2.63%	5.89%	
Other Current Liabilities	1.48%	1.46%	2.50%	1.04%	1.16%	
Total Current Liabilities	17.04%	21.27%	29.66%	21.58%	25.52%	
Long-Term Debt	0.00%	0.00%	0.00%	20.09%	6.37%	
Pension & Other Post-Retire. Benefits	0.00%	0.00%	0.00%	0.33%	0.46%	
Other Non-Current Liabilities	11.01%	11.63%	10.93%	10.63%	13.63%	
Total Liabilities	28.05%	32.90%	40.58%	52.63%	45.97%	
Common Stock	0.07%	0.09%	0.08%	0.06%	0.07%	
Additional Paid in Capital	84.29%	71.19%	58.85%	44.47%	49.68%	
Retained Earnings	(12.40)%	(4.19)%	0.49%	2.84%	4.28%	
Treasury Stock	0.00%	0.00%	0.00%	0.00%	0.00%	
Comprehensive Inc. and Other	0.00%	0.00%	0.00%	0.00%	0.00%	
Total Common Equity	71.95%	67.10%	59.42%	47.37%	54.03%	
Total Equity	71.95%	67.10%	59.42%	47.37%	54.03%	
Total Liabilities and Equity	100.00%	100.00%	100.00%	100.00%	100.00%	
Supplemental Items						
Total Shares Out. on Balance Sheet Date	10.76%	9.32%	7.72%	6.48%	6.91%	
Total Debt	0.00%	0.00%	5.72%	20.09%	6.37%	
Net Debt	(8.28)%	(2.64)%	2.78%	16.18%	0.25%	
Debt Equivalent Oper. Leases	66.64%	70.59%	68.86%	82.52%	87.02%	75%
Land	2.11%	1.86%	1.58%	1.57%	1.65%	
Buildings	86.60%	3.24%	2.74%	2.87%	3.22%	
Machinery	50.85%	48.91%	47.58%	53.41%	54.94%	
Construction in Progress	6.03%	13.03%	10.19%	9.67%	1.82%	
Leasehold Improvements	82.93%	83.65%	85.97%	92.90%	110.52%	91%

3. The common size form of the Income Statement.

Cracker Barrel Old Country Store, Inc. (NasdaqGS:CBRL)
In Millions of USD, except per share items.

			Income Statement		
For the Fiscal Period Ending	Reclassified Jul-28-2006	Reclassified Aug-03-2007	Aug-01-2008	Jul-31-2009	Jul-30-2010
Total Revenue	100.00%	100.00%	100.00%	100.00%	100.00%
Cost of Goods Sold	69.34%	69.62%	70.59%	71.02%	68.79%
Gross Profit	30.66%	30.38%	29.41%	28.98%	31.21%
Selling General & Admin. Exp.	23.07%	23.29%	23.05%	22.89%	24.25%
R & D Exp.	0.00%	0.00%	0.00%	0.00%	0.00%
Depreciation & Amort.	0.00%	0.00%	0.00%	0.00%	0.00%
Other Operating Expense/(Income)	0.00%	0.00%	0.00%	0.00%	0.00%
Other Operating Exp., Total	23.07%	23.29%	23.05%	22.89%	24.25%
Operating Income	7.59%	7.09%	6.36%	6.10%	6.96%
Interest Expense	(1.00)%	(2.53)%	(2.41)%	(2.21)%	(2.04)%
Interest and Invest. Income	0.03%	0.33%	0.01%	0.00%	0.00%
Net Interest Exp.	(0.96)%	(2.20)%	(2.40)%	(2.21)%	(2.04)%
Other Non-Operating Inc. (Exp.)	0.00%	0.00%	0.00%	0.00%	0.00%
EBT Excl. Unusual Items	6.62%	4.90%	3.96%	3.89%	4.93%
Restructuring Charges	(0.30)%	0.00%	0.00%	0.00%	0.00%
Impairment of Goodwill	0.00%	0.00%	0.00%	0.00%	0.00%
Asset Writedown	0.00%	0.00%	(0.04)%	(0.09)%	(0.12)%
Legal Settlements	0.00%	0.06%	0.00%	0.00%	0.00%
Other Unusual Items	0.00%	0.00%	0.00%	0.00%	0.00%
EBT Incl. Unusual Items	6.32%	4.95%	3.92%	3.80%	4.81%
Income Tax Expense	2.02%	1.72%	1.18%	1.02%	1.27%
Earnings from Cont. Ops.	4.30%	3.23%	2.74%	2.79%	3.55%
Earnings of Discontinued Ops.	0.94%	3.66%	0.01%	0.00%	0.00%
Extraord. Item & Account. Change	0.00%	0.00%	0.00%	0.00%	0.00%
Net Income	5.24%	6.89%	2.75%	2.78%	3.55%
Dividends per Share	0.02%	0.02%	0.03%	0.03%	0.03%
Payout Ratio %	0.01%	0.00%	0.01%	0.01%	0.01%

	Income Statement				
For the Fiscal Period Ending	Reclassified Jul-28-2006	Reclassified Aug-03-2007	Aug-01-2008	Jul-31-2009	Jul-30-2010
Supplemental Items					
EBITDA	10.17%	9.51%	8.78%	8.60%	9.50%
EBITA	7.59%	7.09%	6.36%	6.10%	6.96%
EBIT	7.59%	7.09%	6.36%	6.10%	6.96%
EBITDAR	12.61%	11.87%	11.21%	11.15%	12.24%
Supplemental Operating Expense Items					
Advertising Exp.	1.72%	1.72%	1.77%	1.79%	1.88%
General and Administrative Exp.	5.80%	5.79%	5.34%	5.08%	6.07%
Net Rental Exp.	2.45%	2.36%	2.43%	2.55%	2.74%
Imputed Oper. Lease Interest Exp.	0.78%	1.35%	1.42%	1.40%	1.59%
Imputed Oper. Lease Depreciation	1.67%	1.01%	1.01%	1.15%	1.15%

Chipotle Mexican Grill, Inc. (NYSE:CMG)
In Millions of USD, except per share items.

	Income Statement				
For the Fiscal Period Ending	Dec-31-2005	Dec-31-2006	Reclassified Dec-31-2007	Reclassified Dec-31-2008	Dec-31-2009
Total Revenue	100%	100.00%	100.00%	100.00%	100.0%
Cost of Goods Sold	68%	66.58%	65.55%	65.95%	63.6%
Gross Profit	32%	33.42%	34.45%	34.05%	36.4%
Selling General & Admin. Exp.	8%	8.26%	9.05%	8.79%	8.2%
Pre-Opening Costs	0%	0.50%	0.46%	0.43%	0.3%
R & D Exp.	0%	0.00%	0.00%	0.00%	0.0%
Depreciation & Amort.	4%	4.16%	4.02%	3.96%	4.0%
Other Operating Expense/(Income)	13%	12.49%	10.40%	10.66%	10.1%
Other Operating Exp., Total	26%	25.40%	23.92%	23.84%	22.6%
Operating Income	5%	8.01%	10.53%	10.21%	13.8%
Interest Expense	0%	(0.04)%	(0.03)%	(0.02)%	0.0%
Interest and Invest. Income	0%	0.80%	0.56%	0.26%	0.1%
Net Interest Exp.	0%	0.77%	0.54%	0.24%	0.0%
Other Non-Operating Inc. (Exp.)	0%	0.00%	0.00%	0.00%	0.0%

(Continued)

Income Statement

For the Fiscal Period Ending	Dec-31-2005	Dec-31-2006	Reclassified Dec-31-2007	Reclassified Dec-31-2008	Dec-31-2009
EBT Excl. Unusual Items	5%	8.78%	11.07%	10.45%	13.8%
Impairment of Goodwill	0%	0.00%	0.00%	0.00%	0.0%
Gain (Loss) on Sale of Assets	0%	(0.49)%	(0.57)%	(0.70)%	(0.4)%
Other Unusual Items	0%	0.00%	0.00%	(0.20)%	0.0%
EBT Incl. Unusual Items	5%	8.29%	10.50%	9.55%	13.4%
Income Tax Expense	(1)%	3.26%	4.00%	3.68%	5.1%
Earnings from Cont. Ops.	6%	5.03%	6.50%	5.87%	8.4%
Earnings of Discontinued Ops.	0%	0.00%	0.00%	0.00%	0.0%
Extraord. Item & Account. Change	0%	0.00%	0.00%	0.00%	0.0%
Net Income	6%	5.03%	6.50%	5.87%	8.4%
Supplemental Items					
EBITDA	10%	12.17%	14.55%	14.17%	17.8%
EBITA	5%	8.01%	10.53%	10.21%	13.8%
EBIT	5%	8.01%	10.53%	10.21%	13.8%
EBITDAR	16%	18.06%	21.00%	21.00%	24.5%
Supplemental Operating Expense Items					
Advertising Exp.	2%	1.69%	0.00%	0.00%	0.0%
Marketing Exp.	0%	0.00%	1.72%	1.66%	1.4%
Selling and Marketing Exp.	0%	0.00%	1.72%	1.66%	1.4%
General and Administrative Exp.	8%	7.93%	6.91%	6.69%	6.5%
Net Rental Exp.	7%	5.89%	6.45%	6.83%	6.7%
Imputed Oper. Lease Interest Exp.	10%	3.34%	3.75%	4.13%	5.5%
Imputed Oper. Lease Depreciation	(4)%	2.55%	2.70%	2.70%	1.2%

Buffalo Wild Wings Inc. (NasdaqGS:BWLD)
In Millions of USD, except per share items.

Income Statement

For the Fiscal Period Ending	Reclassified Dec-25-2005	Reclassified Dec-31-2006	Dec-30-2007	Dec-28-2008	Dec-27-2009
Total Revenue	100.00%	100.00%	100.00%	100.00%	100.00%
Cost of Goods Sold	75.38%	74.67%	74.57%	74.15%	74.77%
Gross Profit	24.62%	25.33%	25.43%	25.85%	25.23%

	Income Statement				
For the Fiscal Period Ending	Reclassified Dec-25-2005	Reclassified Dec-31-2006	Dec-30-2007	Dec-28-2008	Dec-27-2009
Selling General & Admin. Exp.	10.64%	10.92%	10.84%	9.51%	9.17%
Pre-Opening Costs	1.24%	1.11%	1.37%	1.88%	1.43%
R & D Exp.		0.00%	0.00%	0.00%	0.00%
Depreciation & Amort.	5.61%	5.21%	5.15%	5.59%	6.05%
Other Operating Expense/(Income)	0.00%	0.00%	0.00%	0.00%	0.00%
Other Operating Exp., Total	17.49%	17.23%	17.37%	16.97%	16.65%
Operating Income	7.14%	8.09%	8.07%	8.87%	8.59%
Interest Expense	0.00%	0.00%	0.00%	0.00%	0.00%
Interest and Invest. Income	0.64%	0.84%	0.88%	0.23%	0.20%
Net Interest Exp.	0.64%	0.84%	0.88%	0.23%	0.20%
Other Non-Operating Inc. (Exp.)	0.00%	0.00%	0.00%	0.00%	0.00%
EBT Excl. Unusual Items	7.78%	8.93%	8.95%	9.10%	8.79%
Restructuring Charges	(0.95)%	(0.36)%	0.00%	0.00%	0.00%
Impairment of Goodwill	0.00%	0.00%	0.00%	0.00%	0.00%
Asset Writedown	0.00%	0.00%	(0.30)%	(0.50)%	(0.35)%
Other Unusual Items	0.00%	0.00%	0.00%	0.00%	0.00%
EBT Incl. Unusual Items	6.83%	8.57%	8.65%	8.61%	8.43%
Income Tax Expense	2.59%	2.72%	2.69%	2.82%	2.74%
Earnings from Cont. Ops.	4.23%	5.85%	5.96%	5.78%	5.69%
Earnings of Discontinued Ops.	0.00%	0.00%	0.00%	0.00%	0.00%
Extraord. Item & Account. Change	0.00%	0.00%	0.00%	0.00%	0.00%
Net Income	4.23%	5.85%	5.96%	5.78%	5.69%
Supplemental Items					
EBITDA	12.79%	13.28%	13.20%	14.46%	14.64%
EBITA	7.18%	8.07%	8.05%	8.92%	8.70%
EBIT	7.14%	8.09%	8.07%	8.87%	8.59%
EBITDAR	18.56%	18.71%	18.46%	19.76%	19.81%
Supplemental Operating Expense Items					
Advertising Exp.	2.77%	3.26%	3.20%	3.20%	3.30%
General and Administrative Exp.	10.64%	10.92%	10.84%	9.51%	9.17%
Net Rental Exp.	5.77%	5.43%	5.26%	5.30%	5.18%

California Pizza Kitchen Inc. (NasdaqGS:CPKI)
In Millions of USD, except per share items.

	Income Statement				
For the Fiscal Period Ending	Jan-01-2006	Dec-31-2006	Dec-30-2007	Dec-28-2008	Jan-03-2010
Total Revenue	100.00%	100.00%	100.00%	100.00%	100.00%
Cost of Goods Sold	80.29%	80.08%	80.12%	81.70%	81.77%
Gross Profit	19.71%	19.92%	19.88%	18.30%	18.23%
Selling General & Admin. Exp.	7.57%	7.81%	7.65%	7.74%	7.88%
Pre-Opening Costs	0.84%	1.26%	1.13%	0.66%	0.28%
R & D Exp.	0.00%	0.00%	0.00%	0.00%	0.00%
Depreciation & Amort.	5.30%	5.32%	5.87%	5.95%	6.05%
Other Operating Expense/(Income)	0.00%	0.00%	0.00%	0.00%	0.00%
Other Operating Exp., Total	13.72%	14.38%	14.65%	14.35%	14.21%
Operating Income	6.00%	5.53%	5.23%	3.95%	4.03%
Interest Expense	0.00%	0.00%	(0.02)%	(0.19)%	(0.12)%
Interest and Invest. Income	0.15%	0.13%	0.00%	0.00%	0.00%
Net Interest Exp.	0.15%	0.13%	(0.02)%	(0.19)%	(0.12)%
Income/(Loss) from Affiliates	0.00%	0.00%	0.00%	0.00%	0.00%
Other Non-Operating Inc. (Exp.)	0.00%	0.00%	0.00%	0.00%	0.00%
EBT Excl. Unusual Items	6.14%	5.66%	5.22%	3.76%	3.91%
Restructuring Charges	(0.04)%	(0.13)%	(1.47)%	(0.15)%	(0.08)%
Impairment of Goodwill	0.00%	0.00%	0.00%	0.00%	0.00%
Asset Writedown	(0.25)%	0.00%	0.00%	(1.96)%	(3.45)%
Legal Settlements	(0.13)%	0.00%	(0.36)%	0.00%	0.00%
Other Unusual Items	0.23%	0.00%	0.00%	0.00%	0.00%
EBT Incl. Unusual Items	5.98%	5.53%	3.39%	1.63%	0.37%
Income Tax Expense	1.91%	1.75%	1.05%	0.35%	(0.32)%
Earnings from Cont. Ops.	4.06%	3.79%	2.34%	1.28%	0.69%
Earnings of Discontinued Ops.	0.00%	0.00%	0.00%	0.00%	0.00%
Extraord. Item & Account. Change	0.00%	0.00%	0.00%	0.00%	0.00%
Net Income	4.06%	3.79%	2.34%	1.28%	0.69%
Supplemental Items					
EBITDA	11.30%	10.85%	11.10%	9.90%	10.07%
EBITA	6.00%	5.53%	5.23%	3.97%	4.04%
EBIT	6.00%	5.53%	5.23%	3.95%	4.03%
EBITDAR	16.06%	15.79%	16.09%	15.52%	15.80%
Supplemental Operating Expense Items					
Advertising Exp.	0.87%	0.88%	0.87%	0.97%	1.11%
General and Administrative Exp.	7.57%	7.81%	7.65%	7.74%	7.88%

	Income Statement				
For the Fiscal Period Ending	Jan-01-2006	Dec-31-2006	Dec-30-2007	Dec-28-2008	Jan-03-2010
Net Rental Exp.	4.76%	4.94%	4.99%	5.61%	5.73%
Imputed Oper. Lease Interest Exp.	0.00%	0.00%	0.00%	2.06%	0.82%
Imputed Oper. Lease Depreciation	0.00%	0.00%	0.00%	3.55%	4.91%

Denny's Corporation (NasdaqCM:DENN)
In Millions of USD, except per share items.

	Income Statement				
For the Fiscal Period Ending	Reclassified Dec-28-2005	Reclassified Dec-27-2006	Restated Dec-26-2007	Restated Dec-31-2008	Dec-30-2009
Total Revenue	100.00%	100.00%	100.00%	100.00%	100.00%
Cost of Goods Sold	71.11%	70.07%	71.21%	68.32%	65.28%
Gross Profit	28.89%	29.93%	28.79%	31.68%	34.72%
Selling General & Admin. Exp.	9.33%	9.69%	10.10%	11.08%	12.72%
R & D Exp.	0.00%	0.00%	0.00%	0.00%	0.00%
Depreciation & Amort.	5.73%	5.56%	5.25%	5.23%	5.32%
Other Operating Expense/(Income)	7.71%	8.21%	7.87%	7.90%	7.09%
Other Operating Exp., Total	22.78%	23.46%	23.22%	24.21%	25.13%
Operating Income	6.11%	6.47%	5.57%	7.47%	9.60%
Interest Expense	(5.80)%	(5.99)%	(4.72)%	(4.83)%	(5.64)%
Interest and Invest. Income	0.17%	0.18%	0.15%	0.17%	0.28%
Net Interest Exp.	(5.64)%	(5.80)%	(4.58)%	(4.67)%	(5.36)%
Other Non-Operating Inc. (Exp.)	0.04%	(0.09)%	(0.06)%	(0.99)%	0.37%
EBT Excl. Unusual Items	0.52%	0.57%	0.93%	1.82%	4.60%
Restructuring Charges	(0.53)%	(0.62)%	(0.73)%	(1.18)%	(0.66)%
Impairment of Goodwill	0.00%	0.00%	0.00%	0.00%	0.00%
Gain (Loss) on Sale of Invest.	0.02%	0.05%	0.05%	(0.22)%	0.16%
Gain (Loss) on Sale of Assets	0.34%	5.71%	4.15%	2.46%	3.20%
Asset Writedown	(0.12)%	(0.27)%	(0.12)%	(0.43)%	(0.16)%
Legal Settlements	(0.85)%	(0.17)%	(0.38)%	(0.30)%	(0.07)%
Other Unusual Items	0.00%	(0.76)%	(0.05)%	0.00%	(0.02)%
EBT Incl. Unusual Items	(0.62)%	4.50%	3.85%	2.14%	7.06%
Income Tax Expense	0.12%	1.48%	0.71%	0.46%	0.23%

(Continued)

Income Statement					
For the Fiscal Period Ending	Reclassified Dec-28-2005	Reclassified Dec-27-2006	Restated Dec-26-2007	Restated Dec-31-2008	Dec-30-2009
Earnings from Cont. Ops.	(0.75)%	3.03%	3.14%	1.68%	6.83%
Earnings of Discontinued Ops.	0.00%	0.00%	0.00%	0.00%	0.00%
Extraord. Item & Account. Change	0.00%	0.02%	0.00%	0.00%	0.00%
Net Income	(0.75)%	3.05%	3.14%	1.68%	6.83%
Supplemental Operating Expense Items					
Selling and Marketing Exp.	2.91%	3.01%	2.92%	3.06%	3.30%
General and Administrative Exp.	6.43%	6.68%	7.17%	8.02%	9.42%
Net Rental Exp.	5.23%	5.10%	5.32%	6.55%	8.03%
Imputed Oper. Lease Interest Exp.	4.30%	4.82%	4.68%	5.66%	7.21%
Imputed Oper. Lease Depreciation	0.94%	0.28%	0.64%	0.89%	0.81%
Maintenance & Repair Exp.	1.91%	1.84%	1.95%	1.92%	1.63%

4. Does the decision to franchise or to own and operate show up in an analysis of the firm's financial statements?

As of March 17, 2010, **California Pizza Kitchen, Inc. (CPKI)** owned, licensed, or franchised *252 locations in 32 states and 9 foreign countries, of which 205 are company-owned and 47 operate under franchise or license arrangements.* The company offers its frozen products to points of distribution through select grocers.

As of December 30, 2009, **Denny's Corporation (DENN)** *operated 1,551 restaurants, including 1,318 franchised/licensed restaurants and 233 company-owned and operated restaurants.*

As of September 21, 2010, **Cracker Barrel Old Country Store**, Inc **(CBRL)** operated 595 full-service restaurants and gift shops in 41 states.

As of June 23, 2010, **Chipotle Mexican Grill, Inc (CMG)** *operated 1,000 restaurants.*

As of December 27, 2009, **Buffalo Wild Wings, Inc *(BWLD)* owned and operated 232 restaurants; and franchised an additional 420** Buffalo Wild Wings Grill & Bar restaurants in 42 states.

Discussion

The five companies show a wide range of operational strategies (franchise or own/operate). However, looking at common form Balance Sheet and Income Statements does not give the analyst a clear picture of the implications of these operational decisions.

The five-year average of items selected to highlight the implications of the operational strategies paints a muddled picture.

	CPKI	DENN	CBRL	CMG	BWLD
Net PP&E	79%	49%	75%	72%	55%
Debt Equivalent Operating Leases	75%	104%	35%	80%	73%
Leasehold Improvements	91%	NR	14%	71%	49%
Gross Profit	19%	31%	30%	34%	25%
Net Income	2%	3%	4%	6%	6%
Advertising Expense	1%	3%	2%	1%	3%

The reader must keep in mind that the decision to own and operate versus franchising is only one of the elements of the business model. For example, CBRL includes gift shops in its stores, CPKI has a line of frozen products distributed via grocers, and BWLD serves wine and beer along with food services.

Finally, the leasing arrangements and the franchising agreements have an important and wide-ranging influence in the financial statements. They should be studied as well in order to present a clear picture of the prospects of the firm.

This illustrates one of the main themes of the approach to financial statement analysis we champion in the book; namely, that mere calculation of ratios and trends is the beginning, not the end of the quest.

5. For the three firms listed below, the stage of growth based an analysis of their financial statements are:

1. L-1 Identity Solutions (ID)

ID is in the growth stage. Sales are increasing at a rapid pace fueled by acquisitions. Operating cash flows are still negligible, and external financing covers most of the investing, which goes to pay for cash acquisitions. Note the large and increasing amounts of goodwill indicating that most of the value of the acquisition comes from intangible capital.

L-1 Identity Solutions Inc. (NYSE:ID)
In Millions of USD, except per share items.

	Analysis (selected items)				
For the Fiscal Period Ending	Dec-31-2005	Dec-31-2006	Dec-31-2007	Dec-31-2008	Dec-31-2009
Total Revenue	66.2	164.4	389.5	562.9	650.9
Gross Profit	23.7	64.7	148.2	192.7	200.1
Selling General & Admin Exp.	19.9	44.4	90.0	123.8	133.9
Net Income	(7.4)	(31.0)	15.8	(551.6)	(4.2)
Cash from Ops.	4.4	12.6	41.0	52.8	60.6
Cash from Investing	(42.9)	(162.4)	(151.9)	(350.9)	(66.2)
Cash from Financing	99.6	82.3	114.1	310.8	(8.5)
Total Debt Issued	0.2	80.0	179.0	295.0	24.9
Total Debt Repaid	(0.3)	(0.3)	(0.8)	(88.8)	(35.1)
Net Interest Exp.	0.2	0.2	(10.9)	(23.1)	(32.7)
Issuance of Common Stock	99.6	7.2	11.9	109.4	2.6
Capital Expenditure	(4.4)	(6.8)	(13.0)	(22.5)	(55.0)
Depreciation & Amort.	6.3	9.1	9.1	18.1	23.5
Cash Acquisitions	(38.7)	(154.7)	(132.8)	(320.5)	(3.7)
Amort. of Goodwill and Intangibles	6.1	14.3	30.1	31.3	13.6
Total Current Assets	92.9	82.0	137.1	181.3	173.1
Total Current Liabilities	15.4	70.3	96.2	156.9	163.7
Net Property, Plant & Equipment	19.5	19.9	23.5	81.3	115.5
Goodwill	152.2	951.4	1,054.3	891.0	889.8
Other Intangibles	27.3	170.1	184.2	108.3	102.4
Additional Paid in Capital	333.5	1,153.8	1,217.8	1,393.8	1,432.9
Retained Earnings	(56.4)	(87.5)	(69.8)	(623.3)	(627.4)
Comprehensive Inc. and Other	(2.4)	0.7	(63.4)	(71.1)	(69.2)
Total Common Equity	274.7	1,067.1	1,084.7	693.4	730.2

2. Aveo Pharmaceuticals (AVEO)

AVEO is in the startup stage. Sales are increasing at an increasing rate. Net Income and Operating Cash Flows are negative. As a pharma/biotech firm, most expenditures are in R&D. Early on the company was financed by issuing debt and preferred stock (Private Equity and/or Venture Capital). In 2010, the company issued an IPO, and the preferred stock was converted to common.

AVEO Pharmaceuticals, Inc. (NasdaqGM:AVEO)
In Millions of USD, except per share items.

Analysis (selected items)

For the Fiscal Period Ending	Dec-31-2006	Dec-31-2007	Dec-31-2008	Dec-31-2009	12 months Sep-30-2010
Total Revenue	7.783	11.034	19.66	20.719	38.761
Gross Profit	5.452	9.009	16.824	17.759	36.001
Selling General & Admin Exp.	5.161	6.502	9.165	10.12	12.815
R & D Exp.	24.514	27.223	38.985	48.832	79.573
Net Income	(24.905)	(24.982)	(32.473)	(44.093)	(59.191)
Total Cash & ST Investments	NA	61.742	32.364	51.301	87.022
Net Property, Plant & Equipment	NA	3.727	3.752	4.197	4.488
Total Assets	NA	67.654	40.087	59.844	96.512
Total Current Liabilities	NA	20.803	19.533	34.305	33.515
Cash from Ops.	(21.716)	(8.604)	(35.301)	(9.973)	(57.827)
Cash from Investing	18.917	(39.894)	28.151	3.414	(26.947)
Cash from Financing	12.84	52.834	6.881	31.035	84.636
Total Debt Issued	14.835	0	20.795	0	7.555
Total Debt Repaid	(2.042)	(4.62)	(13.948)	(1.986)	(4.039)
Issuance of Common Stock	0.047	0.078	0.034	0.159	81.12
Issuance of Pref. Stock	0	57.497	0	0	0.063
Total Shares Out. on Balance Sheet Date	1.33	1.434	1.586	1.641	30.935

3. United Therapeutics (UTHR)

UTHR is in the established growth stage. Sales are increasing fueled by organic growth. Capital expenditures are significant and growing. Net Income and Operating Cash Flows are becoming positive and significant. Of particular interest is the issuance of debt to repurchase stock, followed by issuance of stock. The mystery is resolved when we bring stock-based compensation into the picture. In what is typical of growth companies, UTHR, attracts high-level executives using stock-based compensation and conserves cash not paid in salaries and bonuses.

United Therapeutics Corp. (NasdaqGS:UTHR)
In Millions of USD, except per share items.

	Analysis				
For the Fiscal Period Ending	Restated Dec-31-2005	Restated Dec-31-2006	Restated Dec-31-2007	Restated Dec-31-2008	Dec-31-2009
Total Revenue	115.9	159.6	210.9	281.5	369.8
Gross Profit	103.6	142.6	188.7	251.4	324.5
Selling General & Admin Exp.	24.7	54.0	99.0	91.2	172.1
R & D Exp.	36.1	57.6	83.4	89.2	122.2
Net Income	65.0	74.0	12.4	(49.3)	19.5
Cash from Ops.	43.2	49.3	48.9	(49.2)	97.6
Cash from Investing	(70.7)	(101.6)	(21.7)	(172.5)	(160.5)
Cash from Financing	14.2	74.1	20.9	213.0	36.5
Capital Expenditure	(6.1)	(15.6)	(38.7)	(124.4)	(95.4)
Depreciation & Amort.	2.1	2.4	2.9	3.9	10.7
Cash Acquisitions	—	—	—	—	(3.6)
Total Debt Issued	—	242.0	—	—	—
Issuance of Common Stock	15.0	14.4	58.3	191.9	32.1
Repurchase of Common Stock	—	(157.7)	(67.1)	—	—
Stock-Based Compensation	1.0	24.1	48.7	28.7	101.0
Tax Benefit from Stock Options	—	(10.8)	(29.6)	(21.1)	(4.4)

6. Du Pont Analysis

Du Pont Analysis of Packaged Foods and Meats

	Industry's 2009 Results				
Company Name	Asset Turnover (×) ×	Return on Sales (%) =	Return on Assets (%) ×	Financial Leverage (×) =	Return on Equity
Campbell Soup Co. (NYSE:CPB)	1.23	10.65%	13.10%	6.01	78.79%
ConAgra Foods, Inc. (NYSE:CAG)	1.05	6.35%	6.69%	2.32	15.52%
Dean Foods Co. (NYSE:DF)	1.42	2.15%	3.06%	5.80	17.77%
General Mills Inc. (NYSE:GIS)	0.79	11.08%	8.80%	3.05	26.83%
Hershey Co. (NYSE:HSY)	1.44	8.23%	11.86%	5.10	60.51%
HJ Heinz Co. (NYSE:HNZ)	1.02	8.26%	8.42%	5.52	46.48%
Hormel Foods Corp. (NYSE:HRL)	1.76	5.67%	9.99%	1.69	16.86%
Kellogg Company (NYSE:K)	1.12	9.64%	10.82%	4.93	53.35%
Kraft Foods Inc. (NYSE:KFT)	0.61	7.48%	4.53%	2.58	11.67%
McCormick & Co. Inc. (NYSE:MKC)	0.94	9.39%	8.85%	2.54	22.46%
Mead Johnson Nutrition Company (NYSE:MJN)	1.37	14.14%	19.30%	(3.07)	(59.21)%
Sara Lee Corp. (NYSE:SLE)	1.28	6.36%	8.12%	3.61	29.28%
The J. M. Smucker Company (NYSE:SJM)	0.58	10.16%	5.92%	1.51	8.93%
Tyson Foods Inc. (NYSE:TSN)	2.47	(1.03)%	(2.53)%	2.39	(6.05)%

Note that while both Tyson Food and Mead Johnson show negative return on equity, the reasons are very different. Tyson Food's negative ROE is a result of a Loss from Operations, while Mead Johnson's negative ROE is a result of negative (accounting) shareholders' equity.

Advanced Battery Technologies, Inc. (NasdaqCM:ABAT)
Ratios (except as noted)

For the Fiscal Period Ending	Dec-31-2005	Dec-31-2006	Dec-31-2007	Dec-31-2008	Dec-31-2009
PROFITABILITY					
Return on Assets %	0.6%	22.1%	21.9%	20.2%	9.0%
Return on Capital %	0.7%	23.9%	22.6%	20.6%	10.0%
Return on Equity %	(2.1)%	49.8%	34.2%	28.5%	20.5%
Return on Common Equity %	(2.1)%	49.8%	34.2%	28.5%	20.5%
Gross Margin %	32.9%	55.0%	43.4%	48.8%	44.7%
SG&A Margin %	29.7%	8.7%	7.5%	7.2%	17.5%
EBITDA Margin %	15.9%	48.4%	36.9%	43.3%	30.7%
EBITA Margin %	3.6%	45.7%	35.0%	41.8%	27.5%
EBIT Margin %	3.2%	45.2%	34.8%	41.6%	26.6%
Earnings from Cont. Ops Margin %	(3.7)%	49.2%	32.0%	35.6%	33.6%
Net Income Margin %	(3.7)%	49.2%	32.0%	35.6%	33.6%
ACTIVITY					
Total Asset Turnover	0.3×	0.8×	1.0×	0.8×	0.5×
Fixed Asset Turnover	0.4×	1.3×	2.4×	3.0×	2.0×
Receivable Turnover	4.3×	4.7×	3.0×	2.9×	3.4×
Inventory Turnover	9.2×	17.9×	22.6×	15.9×	13.0×
LIQUIDITY					
Current Ratio	0.5×	8.1×	11.8×	39.5×	17.0×
Quick Ratio	0.3×	5.7×	10.3×	36.8×	14.5×
Avg. Days Sales Out.	84.6	77.2	120.0	124.5	106.6
Avg. Days Inventory Out.	39.6	20.4	16.2	23.0	28.2
Avg. Days Payable Out.	63.8	40.0	10.0	6.3	5.3
Avg. Cash Conversion Cycle	60.4	57.5	126.2	141.2	129.4
LEVERAGE					
Total Debt/Equity	45.3%	1.7%	3.1%	0.0%	2.2%
Total Debt/Capital	27.3%	1.6%	3.0%	0.0%	2.2%
LT Debt/Equity	NA	1.7%	1.1%	NA	NA
LT Debt/Capital	NA	1.6%	1.1%	NA	NA
Total Liabilities/Total Assets	47.0%	5.6%	5.8%	1.7%	16.4%

For the Fiscal Period Ending	Dec-31-2005	Dec-31-2006	Dec-31-2007	Dec-31-2008	Dec-31-2009
COVERAGE					
EBIT / Interest Exp.	0.7×	31.1×	NA	NA	33.7×
EBITDA / Interest Exp.	3.4×	33.3×	NA	NA	39.0×
(EBITDA-CAPEX) / Interest Exp.	NM	32.9×	NA	NA	20.3×
Total Debt/EBITDA	6.1×	0.0×	0.1×	0.0×	0.1×
Net Debt/EBITDA	6.1×	0.0×	NM	NM	NM
Total Debt/ (EBITDA-CAPEX)	NM	0.0×	0.1×	0.0×	0.3×
Net Debt/(EBITDA-CAPEX)	NM	0.0×	NM	NM	NM

Computational Exercises

THE ARITHMETIC OF GROWTH VALUATIONS

Case 1

A corporation is currently reporting annual net earnings of $30.0 million. Assume that five years from now, when its growth has leveled off somewhat, the corporation will be valued at 15 times earnings.

Further assume that the company will pay no dividends over the next five years and that investors in growth stocks currently seek returns of 25 percent (before considering capital gains taxes). Suppose the corporation's earnings have been growing at a 15 percent annual rate and appear likely to continue increasing at the same rate over the next five years.

No dividends for the next five years

		Year	Earnings	Valuation	Present Value
Current Net Earnings		0	30.0		
Growth Rate	15%	1	34.5		
Required Rate	25%	2	39.7		
		3	45.6		
		4	52.5		
Multiple	15	5	60.3	905.1107	296.6
Owner's Share	20%				59.3

		Year	Earnings	Valuation	Present Value
Current Net Earnings		0	30.0		
Growth Rate	25%	1	37.5		
Required Rate	25%	2	46.9		
		3	58.6		
		4	73.2		
Multiple	15	5	91.6	1,373.3000	450.0
Owner's Share	20%				90.0
				Difference	30.7

At the end of that period, earnings (rounded) will be *$60.3* million annually. Applying a multiple of 15 times to that figure produces a valuation at the end of the fifth year of *$905.1* million. Investors seeking a 25 percent rate of return will pay *$296.6* million today for that future value.

Say the founder still owns 20 percent of the shares outstanding, which means she is worth *$59.3* million. Suppose investors conclude for some reason that the corporation's potential for increasing its earnings has changed from 15 to 25 percent per annum.

The value of corporation's shares will change from *$296.6* million to *$450.0* million, keeping previous assumptions intact. Now the founder's shares are worth *$90.0* million, a difference of *$30.7*.

Case 2

A corporation is currently reporting annual net earnings of $20.0 million. Assume that five years from now, when its growth has leveled off somewhat, the corporation will be valued at 20 times earnings.

Further assume that the company will pay no dividends over the next five years and that investors in growth stocks currently seek returns of 22 percent (before considering capital gains taxes). Suppose the corporation's earnings have been growing at a 20 percent annual rate and appear likely to continue increasing at the same rate over the next five years.

At the end of that period, earnings (rounded) will be *$49.8* million annually. Applying a multiple of 20 times to that figure produces a valuation at the end of the fifth year of *$995.3* million. Investors seeking a 22 percent rate of return will pay *$368.3* million today for that future value.

Say the founder still owns 40 percent of the shares outstanding, which means she is worth *$147.3* million. Suppose investors conclude for some reason that the corporation's potential for increasing its earnings has changed from 20 to 18 percent per annum.

The value of corporation's shares will change from *$368.3* million to *$338.6* million, keeping previous assumptions intact. Now the founder's shares are worth *$135.4* million, a difference of *$(11.9)*.

No dividends for the next five years

		Year	Earnings	Valuation	Present Value
Current Net Earnings		0	20.0		
Growth Rate	20%	1	24.0		
Required Rate	22%	2	28.8		

		Year	Earnings	Valuation	Present Value
		3	34.6		
		4	41.5		
Multiple	20	5	49.8	995.3	368.3
Owner's Share	40%				147.3
		Year	**Earnings**	**Valuation**	**Present Value**
Current Net Earnings		0	20.0		
Growth Rate	18%	1	23.6		
Required Rate	22%	2	27.8		
		3	32.9		
		4	38.8		
Multiple	20	5	45.8	915.1	338.6
Owner's Share	40%				135.4
				Difference	(11.9)

Case 3

A corporation is currently reporting annual net earnings of $20.0 million. Assume that five years from now, when its growth has leveled off somewhat, the corporation will be valued at 12 times earnings.

Further assume that the company will pay no dividends over the next five years and that investors in growth stocks currently seek returns of 25 percent (before considering capital gains taxes). Suppose the corporation's earnings have been growing at a 10 percent annual rate and appear likely to continue increasing at the same rate over the next five years.

At the end of that period, earnings (rounded) will be *$32.2* million annually. Applying a multiple of 12 times to that figure produces a valuation at the end of the fifth year of *$386.5* million. Investors seeking a 25 percent rate of return will pay *$126.7* million today for that future value.

Say the founder still owns 20 percent of the shares outstanding, which means she is worth *$25.3* million. Suppose investors conclude for some reason that the corporation's potential for increasing its earnings has changed from 10 to 20 percent per annum.

The value of corporation's shares will change from *$126.7* million to *$195.7* million, keeping previous assumptions intact. Now the founder's shares are worth *$39.1* million, a difference of *$13.8*.

No dividends for the next five years

		Year	Earnings	Valuation	Present Value
Current Net Earnings		0	20.0		
Growth Rate	10%	1	22.0		
Required Rate	25%	2	24.2		
		3	26.6		
		4	29.3		
Multiple	12	5	32.2	386.5	126.7
Owner's Share	20%				25.3

		Year	Earnings	Valuation	Present Value
Current Net Earnings		0	20.0		
Growth Rate	20%	1	24.0		
Required Rate	25%	2	28.8		
		3	34.6		
		4	41.5		
Multiple	12	5	49.8	597.2	195.7
Owner's Share	20%				39.1
				Difference	13.8

Case 4

A corporation is currently reporting annual net earnings of $20.0 million. Assume that five years from now, when its growth has leveled off somewhat, the corporation will be valued at 20 times earnings.

Further assume that the company will pay no dividends over the next five years and that investors in growth stocks currently seek returns of 22 percent (before considering capital gains taxes). Suppose the corporation's earnings have been growing at a 12 percent annual rate and appear likely to continue increasing at the same rate over the next five years.

At the end of that period, earnings (rounded) will be *$35.2* million annually. Applying a multiple of 20 times to that figure produces a valuation at the end of the fifth year of *$704.9* million. Investors seeking a 22 percent rate of return will pay *$260.8* million today for that future value.

No dividends for the next five years

		Year	Earnings	Valuation	Present Value
Current Net Earnings		0	20.0		
Growth Rate	12%	1	22.4		

		Year	Earnings	Valuation	Present Value
Required Rate	22%	2	25.1		
		3	28.1		
		4	31.5		
Multiple	20	5	35.2	704.9	260.8
Owner's Share	40%				104.3
		Year	Earnings	Valuation	Present Value
Current Net Earnings		0	20.0		
Growth Rate	18%	1	23.6		
Required Rate	22%	2	27.8		
		3	32.9		
		4	38.8		
Multiple	20	5	45.8	915.1	338.6
Owner's Share	40%				135.4
				Difference	31.1

Say the founder still owns 40 percent of the shares outstanding, which means she is worth *$104.3* million. Suppose investors conclude for some reason that the corporation's potential for increasing its earnings has changed from 12 to 18 percent per annum.

The value of corporation's shares will change from *$260.8* million to *$338.6* million, keeping previous assumptions intact. Now the founder's shares are worth *$135.4* million, a difference of *$31.1.*

MARKET VALUE VERSUS BOOK VALUE OF BONDS

This is an example of how a Liability can be an Asset. Long-term bonds that are carried in the books at face value in the Liability side of the balance sheet, are, in fact, an asset when the their market value is above the their face value.

Market Value versus Book Value of Debt

		Period	Cash Flow	Present Value
Face Value	$20,000,000	0		
Maturity (Years)	8	1	$1,212,500	1,124,090

(Continued)

			Period	Cash Flow	Present Value
Coupon Rate	12.125%		2	$ 1,212,500	1,042,127
Yield	15.730%		3	$ 1,212,500	966,140
			4	$ 1,212,500	895,694
Price	$16,781,355		5	$ 1,212,500	830,384
			6	$ 1,212,500	769,836
Bond Price =	$16,781,355		7	$ 1,212,500	713,704
Present Value					
of Coupons		$10,825,540	8	$ 1,212,500	661,664
Present Value					
of Principal		$ 5,955,815	9	$ 1,212,500	613,418
		$16,781,355	10	$ 1,212,500	568,691
			11	$ 1,212,500	527,225
Difference	$ 3,218,645		12	$ 1,212,500	488,782
			13	$ 1,212,500	453,142
			14	$ 1,212,500	420,101
			15	$ 1,212,500	389,470
			16	$ 1,212,500	361,071
			16	$20,000,000	5,955,815
				Bond Price	16,781,355

Case 1

A firm shows in its books bonds with a face value of $20,000,000. The bonds were issued at par, with a semi-annual coupon rate of 12.125 percent, and now have eight years to maturity. However, the bonds are now priced to yield 15.730 percent. The market value of this long-term obligation is *$16,781,355* and the difference between the market value and the book value of the bond is *$3,218,645.*

Case 2

A firm shows in its books bonds with a face value of $50,000,000. The bonds were issued at par, with a semi-annual coupon rate of 14.125 percent, and now have eight years to maturity. However, the bonds are now priced to yield 10.500 percent. The market value of this long-term obligation is *$16,781,355,* and the difference between the market value and the book value of the bond is *$(9,649,269).*

Market Value versus Book Value of Debt

			Period	Cash Flow	Present Value
Face Value	$50,000,000		0		
Maturity (Years)	8		1	$ 3,531,250	3,355,107
Coupon Rate	14.125%		2	$ 3,531,250	3,187,750
Yield	10.500%		3	$ 3,531,250	3,028,741
			4	$ 3,531,250	2,877,664
Price	$59,649,269		5	$ 3,531,250	2,734,122
			6	$ 3,531,250	2,597,741
Bond Price =	$59,649,269		7	$ 3,531,250	2,468,162
Present Value of Coupons		$37,598,876	8	$ 3,531,250	2,345,047
Present Value of Principal		$22,050,393	9	$ 3,531,250	2,228,074
		$59,649,269	10	$ 3,531,250	2,116,934
			11	$ 3,531,250	2,011,339
Difference	$ (9,649,269)		12	$ 3,531,250	1,911,011
			13	$ 3,531,250	1,815,688
			14	$ 3,531,250	1,725,119
			15	$ 3,531,250	1,639,068
			16	$ 3,531,250	1,557,309
			16	$50,000,000	22,050,393
				Bond Price	59,649,269

Case 3

A firm shows in its books bonds with a face value of $35,000,000. The bonds were issued at par, with a semi-annual coupon rate of 6.000 percent, and now have eight years to maturity. However, the bonds are now priced to yield 10.000 percent. The market value of this long-term obligation is *$16,781,355*, and the difference between the market value and the book value of the bond is *$7,586,439*.

Market Value versus Book Value of Debt

		Period	Cash Flow	Present Value
Face Value	$35,000,000	0		
Maturity (Years)	8	1	$ 1,050,000	1,000,000

(Continued)

			Period	Cash Flow	Present Value
Coupon Rate	6.000%		2	$ 1,050,000	952,381
Yield	10.000%		3	$ 1,050,000	907,029
			4	$ 1,050,000	863,838
Price	$27,413,561		5	$ 1,050,000	822,702
			6	$ 1,050,000	783,526
Bond Price =	$27,413,561		7	$ 1,050,000	746,215
Present Value					
of Coupons		$11,379,658	8	$ 1,050,000	710,681
Present Value					
of Principal		$16,033,903	9	$ 1,050,000	676,839
		$27,413,561	10	$ 1,050,000	644,609
			11	$ 1,050,000	613,913
Difference	$ 7,586,439		12	$ 1,050,000	584,679
			13	$ 1,050,000	556,837
			14	$ 1,050,000	530,321
			15	$ 1,050,000	505,068
			16	$ 1,050,000	481,017
			16	$35,000,000	16,033,903
				Bond Price	27,413,561

ACQUISITIONS DRIVEN BY P/E MULTIPLES

Case 1

Big Time Corp.'s sales increase by 10.0 percent between Year 1 and Year 2. Small Change, a smaller, privately owned company in the same industry, also achieves 10.0 percent year-over-year sales growth. Suppose now that at the end of Year 1, Big Time acquires Small Change with shares of its own stock. The Big Time income statements under this assumption ("Acquisition Scenario") show a *15.2 percent* sales increase between Year 1 and Year 2.

On the face of it, a company growing at *15.2 percent* a year is sexier than one growing at only 10.0 percent a year. Observe, however, that Big Time's profitability, measured by net income as a percentage of sales, does not improve as a result of the acquisition. Combining two companies with equivalent profit margins of *3.0 percent* produces a larger company that also earns *3.0 percent* on sales. Shareholders do not gain anything in the process, as the following figures demonstrate.

If Big Time decides not to acquire Small Change, its number of shares outstanding remains at 125.0 million. The earnings increase from *$150.0* million in Year 1 to $165.0 million in Year 2 raises earnings-per-share from $1.20 to $1.32. With the price-earnings multiple at 12 times, equivalent to the average of the company's industry peers, Big Time's stock price rises from $14.40 to $15.84 a share.

In the Acquisition Scenario, on the other hand, Big Time pays its industry-average earnings multiple of 12 times for Small Change, for a total acquisition price of $85.5 million. At Big Time's Year 1 share price of $14.40, the purchase therefore requires the issuance of 5.9 million shares.

With the addition of Small Change's net income, Big Time earns $172.9 million in Year 2. Dividing that figure by the increased number of shares outstanding (130.9 million) produces earnings per share of $1.32. At a price-earnings multiple of 12 times, Big Time is worth $15.84 a share, precisely the price calculated in the Non-Acquisition Scenario.

The mere increase in annual sales growth from 10.0 percent to 15.2 percent has not benefited shareholders, whose shares increase in value by 10 percent whether Big Time acquires Small Change or not.

Acquisitions Driven by P/E Multiples
Big Time Corp. and Small Change Inc.

		Non-Acquisition Scenario				Acquisition Scenario	
		Big Time Corp		Small Change Inc.		Big Time Corp	
		Year 1	Year 2	Year 1	Year 2	Year 1	Year 2
Debt		$1,000.00	$1,100.00	32.00	$ 35.20	$1,000.00	1,032.00
Equity		$1,000.00	$1,100.00	25.00	$ 27.50	$1,000.00	
Big Time Annual Coupon Rate for Debt	10%						
Small Change Annual Coupon Rate for Debt	15%						
($000.000 Omitted)							
Sales		$5,000.00	$5,500.00	$238.10	$261.90	$5,000.00	$5,761.90
Cost and Expenses							
Cost of Goods Sold		3,422.70	3,765.00	160.60	176.70	$3,422.70	3,941.60
Selling, General, and Administrative Expenses		1,250.00	$1,375.00	61.90	68.10	$1,250.00	1,443.10

(Continued)

	Non-Acquisition Scenario				Acquisition Scenario	
	Big Time Corp		Small Change Inc.		Big Time Corp	
	Year 1	Year 2	Year 1	Year 2	Year 1	Year 2
Interest Expense	100.00	110.00	4.80	5.30	$ 100.00	115.30
Total Costs and Expenses	4,772.70	5,250.00	227.30	250.00	$4,772.70	5,500.00
Income before Income Tax Expenses	227.30	250.00	10.80	11.90	$1,227.30	261.90
Income Taxes	77.30	85.00	3.70	4.00	77.30	89.00
Net Income	$ 150.00	$ 165.00	$ 7.10	7.80	$ 150.00	$ 172.90
Year-over-Year Sales Increase		10.00%		10.00%		15.20%
Net Income as a Percentage of Sales	3.00%	3.00%	3.00%	3.00%	3.00%	3.00%
Shares Outstanding (million)	125.00	125.00			125.00	130.90
Earnings per Share	$ 1.20	$ 1.32			$ 1.20	$ 1.32
Price-Earnings Multiple (times)	12.00	12.00	12.00	12.00	12.00	12.00
Price per Share	$ 114.40	$ 15.84			$ 14.40	$ 15.84
Year-over-Year Increase		10.00%				10.00%
Market Capitalization	$1,800.20	$1,980.20	$ 85.50	$ 94.10	$1,800.20	$2,074.30
Year-over-Year Increase		10.00%		10.00%		15.00%
Debt/Equity Ratio	55.50%	55.50%	37.40%	37.40%	55.50%	49.80%
Acquisition Price				$85.50		
Number of Shares				5.90		
taxrate	34%					
growth_rate	10%					
industry_PE_ mult	12					

Case 2

Big Time Corp.'s sales increase by 8.0 percent between Year 1 and Year 2. Small Change, a smaller, privately owned company in the same industry, also achieves 8.0 percent year-over-year sales growth. Suppose now that at the end of Year 1, Big Time acquires Small Change with shares of its own stock. The Big Time income statements under this assumption ("Acquisition Scenario") show a *13.1 percent* sales increase between Year 1 and Year 2.

On the face of it, a company growing at *13.1 percent* a year is sexier than one growing at only 8.0 percent a year. Observe, however, that Big Time's profitability, measured by net income as a percentage of sales, does not improve as a result of the acquisition. Combining two companies with equivalent profit margins of *3.0 percent* produces a larger company that also earns *3.0 percent* on sales. Shareholders do not gain anything in the process, as the following figures demonstrate.

If Big Time decides not to acquire Small Change, its number of shares outstanding remains at 125.0 million. The earnings increase from *$150.0* million in Year 1 to *$162.0* million in Year 2 raises earnings-per-share from *$1.20* to *$1.30*. With the price-earnings multiple at 12 times, equivalent to the average of the company's industry peers, Big Time's stock price rises from *$19.20* to *$20.74* a share.

In the Acquisition Scenario, on the other hand, Big Time pays its industry-averager earnings multiple of 16 times for Small Change, for a total acquisition price of *$114.0* million. At Big Time's Year 1 share price of *$19.20*, the purchase therefore requires the issuance of *5.9* million shares. With the addition of Small Change's net income, Big Time earns *$169.7* million in Year 2. Dividing that figure by the increased number of shares outstanding (*130.9* million) produces earnings per share of *$1.30*. At a price-earnings multiple of 16 times, Big Time is worth *$20.74* a share, precisely the price calculated in the Non-Acquisition Scenario.

The mere increase in annual sales growth from 8.0% to *13.1 percent* has not benefited shareholders, whose shares increase in value by *8 percent* whether Big Time acquires Small Change or not.

Acquisitions Driven by P/E Multiples
Big Time Corp. and Small Change Inc

Debt	$1,000.00	$1,080.00	32.00	$ 34.60	$1,000.00	1,032.00
Equity	$1,000.00	$1,080.00	25.00	$ 27.00	$1,000.00	
Big Time Annual Coupon Rate for Debt	10%					
Small Change Annual Coupon Rate for Debt	15%					
($000.000 Omitted)						

(Continued)

| | Non-Acquisition Scenario | | | | Acquisition Scenario | |
| | Big Time Corp | | Small Change Inc. | | Big Time Corp | |
	Year 1	Year 2	Year 1	Year 2	Year 1	Year 2
Sales	$5,000.00	$5,400.00	$238.10	$257.10	$5,000.00	$5,657.10
Cost and Expenses						
Cost of Goods Sold	3,422.70	3,696.50	160.60	173.40	$3,422.70	3,870.00
Selling, General, and Administrative Expenses	1,250.00	$1,350.00	61.90	66.90	$1,250.00	1,416.90
Interest Expense	100.00	108.00	4.80	5.20	$ 100.00	113.20
Total Costs and Expenses	4,772.70	5,154.50	227.30	245.50	$4,772.70	5,400.00
Income before Income Tax Expenses	227.30	245.50	10.80	11.70	$ 227.30	257.10
Income Taxes	77.30	83.50	3.70	4.00	77.30	87.40
Net Income	$ 150.00	$ 162.00	$ 7.10	7.70	$1,150.00	$ 169.70
Year-over-Year Sales Increase		8.00%		8.00%		13.10%
Net Income as a Percentage of Sales	3.00%	3.00%	3.00%	3.00%	3.00%	3.00%
Shares Outstanding (million)	125.00	125.00			125.00	130.90
Earnings per Share	$ 1.20	$ 1.30			$ 1.20	$ 1.30
Price-Earnings Multiple (times)	16.00	16.00	16.00	16.00	16.00	16.00
Price per Share	$ 19.20	$ 20.74			$ 19.20	$ 20.74
Year-over-Year Increase		8.00%				8.00%
Market Capitalization	$2,400.30	$2,592.30	$114.00	$123.20	$2,400.30	$2,715.50
Year-over-Year Increase		8.00%		8.00%		13.00%
Debt/Equity Ratio	41.70%	41.70%	28.10%	28.10%	41.70%	8.00%
Acquisition Price				$114.00		
Number of Shares				5.90		
taxrate	34%					
Growth rate	8%					
industry_PE_ mult.	16					

Case 3

Big Time Corp.'s sales increase by 16.0 percent between Year 1 and Year 2. Small Change, a smaller, privately owned company in the same industry, also achieves 16.0 percent year-over-year sales growth. Suppose now that at the end of Year 1, Big Time acquires Small Change with shares of its own stock. The Big Time income statements under this assumption ("Acquisition Scenario") show a *21.5 percent* sales increase between Year 1 and Year 2.

On the face of it, a company growing at *21.5 percent* a year is sexier than one growing at only 16.0 percent a year. Observe, however, that Big Time's profitability, measured by net income as a percentage of sales, does not improve as a result of the acquisition. Combining two companies with equivalent profit margins of *3.0 percent* produces a larger company that also earns *3.0 percent* on sales. Shareholders do not gain anything in the process, as the figures below demonstrate.

If Big Time decides not to acquire Small Change, its number of shares outstanding remains at 125.0 million. The earnings increase from *$150.0* million in Year 1 to *$174.0* million in Year 2 raises earnings-per-share from *$1.20* to *$1.39*. With the price-earnings multiple at 24 percent times, equivalent to the average of the company's industry peers, Big Time's stock price rises from *$28.80* to *$33.41* a share.

In the Acquisition Scenario, on the other hand, Big Time pays its industry-average earnings multiple of 24 times for Small Change, for a total acquisition price of *$171.1* million. At Big Time's Year 1 share price of *$28.80,* the purchase therefore requires the issuance of *$5.9* million shares. With the addition of Small Change's net income, Big Time earns *$182.3* million in Year 2. Dividing that figure by the increased number of shares outstanding (*130.9* million) produces earnings per share of *$1.39*. At a price-earnings multiple of 24 times, Big Time is worth *$33.41* a share, precisely the price calculated in the Non-Acquisition Scenario.

The mere increase in annual sales growth from 16.0 percent to 21.5 percent has not benefited shareholders, whose shares increase in value by *16 percent* whether Big Time acquires Small Change or not.

Acquisitions Driven by P/E Multiples
Big Time Corp. and Small Change Inc.

Debt	$1,000.00	$1,160.00	32.00	$ 37.60	$1,000.00	1,032.00
Equity	$1,000.00	$1,160.00	25.00	$ 29.00	$1,000.00	
Big Time Annual Coupon Rate for						
Debt	10%					

(Continued)

Small Change Annual Coupon Rate for Debt 15% ($000.000 Omitted)	Non-Acquisition Scenario				Acquisition Scenario	
	Big Time Corp		Small Change Inc.		Big Time Corp	
	Year 1	Year 2	Year 1	Year 2	Year 1	Year 2
Sales	$5,000.00	$5,800.00	$238.10	$276.20	$5,000.00	$6,076.20
Cost and Expenses						
Cost of Goods Sold	3,422.70	3,970.30	160.60	186.30	$3,422.70	4,156.60
Selling, General, and Administrative Expenses	1,250.00	$1,450.00	61.90	71.80	$1,250.00	1,521.80
Interest Expense	100.00	116.00	4.80	5.60	$ 100.00	121.60
Total Costs and Expenses	4,772.70	5,536.30	227.30	263.70	$4,772.70	5,800.00
Income before Income Tax Expenses	227.30	263.70	10.80	12.50	$ 227.30	276.20
Income Taxes	77.30	89.60	3.70	4.30	77.30	93.90
Net Income	$ 150.00	$ 174.00	$ 7.10	8.30	$ 150.00	$ 182.30
Year-over-Year Sales Increase		16.00%		16.00%		21.50%
Net Income as a Percentage of Sales	3.00%	3.00%	3.00%	3.00%	3.00%	3.00%
Shares Outstanding (million)	125.00	125.00			125.00	130.90
Earnings per Share	$ 1.20	$ 1.39			$ 11.20	$ 1.39
Price-Earnings Multiple (times)	24.00	24.00	24.00	24.00	24.00	24.00
Price per Share	$ 28.80	$ 33.41			$ 28.80	$ 33.41
Year-over-Year Increase		16.00%				16.00%
Market Capitalization	$3,600.40	$4,176.50	$171.10	$198.40	$3,600.40	$4,374.90
Year-over-Year Increase		16.00%		16.00%		22.00%
Debt/Equity Ratio	27.80%	27.80%	18.70%	18.70%	27.80%	23.60%
Acquisition Price				$171.10		
Number of Shares				5.90		
taxrate 34%						
growth_rate 16%						
industry_PE_ mult 24						

STOCK PRICES AND GOODWILL

Case 1

The shares of Amalgamator and Consolidator are both trading at multiples of 2.5 times book value per share. Shareholders' equity is $200 million at Amalgamators and $60 million at Consolidator. Amalgamator uses stock held in its treasury to acquire Consolidator for *$263* million.

The purchase price represents a premium of 75 percent above the prevailing market price. Prior to the acquisition, Amalgamator's ratio of total assets to total liabilities is *1.25* times, while the comparable figure for Consolidator is *1.18* times.

The total-assets-to-total-liabilities ratio after the deal is *1.41* times. By paying a premium to Consolidator's tangible asset value, Amalgamator creates *$203* million of goodwill.

Case 2

As the scene opens, an explosive stock market rally has driven up both companies' shares to 4.5 times book value. The ratio of total assets to total liabilities, however, remains at *1.25* times for Amalgamator and *1.18* times for Consolidator. As in Case 1, Amalgamator pays a premium of 75 percent above the prevailing market price to acquire Consolidator.

The premium is calculated on a higher market capitalization, however. Consequently, the purchase price rises from *$263* million to *$473* million. Instead of creating *$203* million of goodwill, the acquisition gives rise to a *$413* million intangible asset. Somehow, putting together a company boasting a *1.25* times ratio with another sporting a *1.18* times ratio has produced an entity with a ratio of *1.59* times.

Now, let us exclude goodwill in calculating the ratio of assets to liabilities. Amalgamator's ratio of tangible assets to total liabilities following its acquisition of Consolidator is *1.23* times in both Case 1 and Case 2. This is the outcome that best reflects economic reality.

	United Amalgamators Corporation	United Consolidators Inc.	Purchase Price	Combined Companies Pro Forma*
Case 1				
Tangible Assets	1,000	400		1,400
Intangible Assets (Goodwill)	0	0		203

(Continued)

	United Amalgamators Corporation	United Consolidators Inc.	Purchase Price	Combined Companies Pro Forma*		
Total Assets	1,000	400		1,603		
Liabilities	800	340		1,140	Premium	75%
Shareholders' Equity (SE)	200	60	263	463		
Total Liabilities and SE	1,000	400		1,603		
					Multiple	2.5
Total Assets/ Total Liabilities	1.25	1.18		1.41		
Tangible Assets/ Total Liabilities	1.25	1.18		1.23		
Market Capitalization	500	150		1,156		
Case 2						
Tangible Assets	1,000	400		1,400		
Intangible Assets (Goodwill)	0	0		413		
Total Assets	1,000	400		1,813		
					Premium	75%
Liabilities	800	340		1,140		
Shareholders' Equity (SE)	200	60	473	673		
Total Liabilities and SE	1,000	400		1,813		
					Rally Multiple	4.5
Total Assets/ Total Liabilities	1.25	1.18		1.59		
Tangible Assets/ Total Liabilities	1.25	1.18		1.23		
Market Capitalization	900	270		3,026		

*Ignores possible impact of EPS dilution.

Case 3

The shares of Amalgamator and Consolidator are both trading at multiples of 1.5 times book value per share. Shareholders' equity is $400 million at Amalgamators and $260 million at Consolidator. Amalgamator uses stock held in its treasury to acquire Consolidator for *$527* million.

The purchase price represents a premium of 35.00 percent above the prevailing market price. Prior to the acquisition, Amalgamator's ratio of total assets to total liabilities is *1.50* times, while the comparable figure for Consolidator is *1.76* times.

The total-assets-to-total-liabilities ratio after the deal is *1.81* times. By paying a premium to Consolidator's tangible asset value, Amalgamator creates $267 million of goodwill.

Case 4

As the scene opens, an explosive stock market rally has driven up both companies' shares to 3.5 times book value. The ratio of total assets to total liabilities, however, remains at *1.50* times for Amalgamator and *1.76* times for Consolidator. As in Case 3, Amalgamator pays a premium of 35.00 percent above the prevailing market price to acquire Consolidator.

The premium is calculated on a higher market capitalization, however. Consequently, the purchase price rises from *$527* million to *$1,229* million. Instead of creating $267 million of goodwill, the acquisition gives rise to a $969 million intangible asset. Somehow, putting together a company boasting a *1.50* times ratio with another sporting a *1.76* times ratio has produced an entity with a ratio of *2.43* times.

Now, let us exclude goodwill in calculating the ratio of assets to liabilities. Amalgamator's ratio of tangible assets to total liabilities following its acquisition of Consolidator is *1.58* times in both Case 3 and Case 4. This is the outcome that best reflects economic reality.

	United Amalgamators Corporation	United Consolidators Inc.	Purchase Price	Combined Companies Pro Forma*
Case 3				
Tangible Assets	1,200	600		1,800
Intangible Assets				
(Goodwill)	0	0		266.5
Total Assets	1,200	600		2,067

(*Continued*)

	United Amalgamators Corporation	United Consolidators Inc.	Purchase Price	Combined Companies Pro Forma*	
Liabilities	800	340		1,140	Premium 35%
Shareholders' Equity (SE)	400	260	527	927	
Total Liabilities and SE	1,200	600		2,067	
					Multiple 1.5
Total Assets/ Total Liabilities	1.5	1.76		1.81	
Tangible Assets/ Total Liabilities	1.5	1.76		1.58	
Market Capitalization	600	390		1,390	
Case 4					
Tangible Assets	1,200	600		1,800	
Intangible Assets (Goodwill)	0	0		969	
Total Assets	1,200	600		2,769	
					Premium 35%
Liabilities	800	340		1,140	
Shareholders' Equity (SE)	400	260	1,229	1,629	
Total Liabilities and SE	1,200	600		2,769	
					Rally 3.5
Total Assets/ Total Liabilities	1.5	1.76		2.43	
Tangible Assets/ Total Liabilities	1.5	1.76		1.58	
Market Capitalization	1,400	910		5,700	

*Ignores possible impact of EPS dilution.

PROJECTING INTEREST EXPENSE

Colossal Chemical Corporation ($000,000 omitted)			
Long-Term Debt (Excluding current maturitites)		2010	2011
Notes Payable			
Due Dates	Rate		
2012	12.000%	82	44
2013	7.500%	56	80
Debentures			
Due Dates			
2018	12.500%	55	55
2020	10.875%	120	120
Industrial Development Bonds			
2023	5.875%	40	40
		$353	$339

($000,000 omitted)						
2010 Amount	2011 Amount	÷2	=	Average Amount Outstanding	@Rate =	Estimated Interest Charges on Long-Term Debt
82	44	2	=	63	12.000% =	$ 7.560
56	80	2	=	68	7.500% =	$ 5.100
55	55	2	=	55	12.500% =	$ 6.875
120	120	2	=	120	10.875% =	$13.050
40	40	2	=	40	5.875% =	$ 2.350
Total				346		$34.935

Interest Charges on Long-Term Debt		Average Amount of Total Long-Term Debt Outstanding		Embedded Cost of Long-Term Debt
$34.935	÷	$346	=	10.100%

Colossal Chemical Corporation ($000,000 omitted)		
Long-Term Debt (Excluding current maturitites)	**2010**	**2011**
Notes Payable		
Due Dates Rate		
2012 9.500%	96	65
2013 9.750%	65	90
Debentures		
Due Dates		
2018 11.880%	50	60
2020 12.125%	90	90
Industrial Development Bonds		
2023 5.125%	60	60
	$361	$365

($000,000 omitted)					
2010 Amount	**2011 Amount**	**÷2 =**	**Average Amount Outstanding**	**@Rate =**	**Estimated Interest Charges on Long-Term Debt**
96	65	2 =	80.5	9.500% =	$ 7.648
65	90	2 =	77.5	9.750% =	$ 7.556
50	60	2 =	55	11.875% =	$ 6.531
90	90	2 =	90	12.125% =	$10.913
60	60	2 =	60	5.125% =	$ 3.075
Total			363		$35.723

Interest Charges on Long-Term Debt		**Average Amount of Total Long-Term Debt Outstanding**		**Embedded Cost of Long-Term Debt**
$35.723	÷	$363	=	9.840%

Colossal Chemical Corporation ($000,000 omitted)			
Long-Term Debt (Excluding current maturitites)		2010	2011
Notes Payable			
Due Dates	Rate		
2012	6.600%	55	75
2013	5.750%	40	60
Debentures			
Due Dates			
2018	10.250%	90	90
2020	9.125%	75	75
Industrial Development Bonds			
2023	8.500%	80	80
		$340	$380

($000,000 omitted)					
2010 Amount	2011 Amount	÷2 =	Average Amount Outstanding	@Rate =	Estimated Interest Charges on Long-Term Debt
55	75	2 =	65	6.600% =	$ 4.290
40	60	2 =	50	5.750% =	$ 2.875
90	90	2 =	90	10.250% =	$ 9.225
75	75	2 =	75	9.125% =	$ 6.844
80	80	2 =	80	8.500% =	$ 6.800
Total			360		$30.034

Interest Charges on Long-Term Debt		Average Amount of Total Long-Term Debt Outstanding		Embedded Cost of Long-Term Debt
$30.034	÷	$360	=	8.340%

SENSITIVITY ANALYSIS IN FORECASTING FINANCIAL STATEMENTS

Impact of Changes in Selected Assumptions on Projected Income Statement

Colossal Chemical Corporation
Year Ended December 31, 2011
($000,000 omitted)

	Base Case	1% Increase in Gross Margin	1% Decline in Tax Rate	5% Increase in Sales
Sales	$2,110	$2,110	$2,110	$2,216
Cost of goods sold	1,161	1,139	1,161	1,219
Selling, general, and administrative expense	$ 528	$ 528	$ 528	$ 554
Depreciation	121	121	121	121
Research and development	84	84	84	84
Total costs and expenses	1,893	1,872	1,893	1,977
Operating Income	$ 217	$ 238	$ 217	$ 238
Interest expense	34	34	34	34
Interest (income)	(5)	(5)	(5)	(5)
Earnings before Income Taxes	$ 188	$ 209	$ 188	$ 209
Provision for Income Taxes	$ 64	$ 71	$ 62	$ 71
Net Income	$ 124	$ 138	$ 126	$ 138
Growth Sales	0%	0%	0%	5%
CGS as % of Sales	55%	54%	55%	55%
SG&A % of Sales	25%	25%	25%	25%
Taxrate	34%	34%	33%	34%

Impact of Changes in Selected Assumptions on Projected Income Statement

Colossal Chemical Corporation
Year Ended December 31, 2011
($000,000 omitted)

	Base Case	1% Increase in Gross Margin	1% Decline in Tax Rate	5% Decrease in Sales
Sales	$2,110	$2,110	$2,110	$2,005
Cost of goods sold	1,161	1,118	1,161	1,102
Selling, general, and administrative expense	$ 528	$ 528	$ 528	$ 501
Depreciation	121	121	121	121
Research and development	84	84	84	84
Total costs and expenses	1,893	1,851	1,893	1,809
Operating Income	$ 217	$ 259	$ 217	$ 196
Interest expense	34	34	34	34
Interest (income)	(5)	(5)	(5)	(5)
Earnings before Income Taxes	$ 188	$ 230	$ 188	$ 167
Provision for Income Taxes	$ 64	$ 78	$ 62	$ 57
Net Income	$ 124	$ 152	$ 126	$ 110

Impact of Changes in Selected Assumptions on Projected
Income Statement

	Colossal Chemical Corporation Year Ended December 31, 2011 ($000,000 omitted)			Change in Sales Growth 5% Change in Gross Margin (2)% Change in SG&A % Sales 5% Taxrate (2)%

	Base Case	Forecast
Sales	$2,110	$2,216
Cost of goods sold	1,161	1,174
Selling, general, and administrative expense	$ 528	$ 665
Depreciation	121	121
Research and development	84	84
Total costs and expenses	1,893	2,044
Operating Income	$ 217	$ 172
Interest expense	34	34
Interest (income)	(5)	(5)
Earnings before Income Taxes	$ 188	$ 143
Provision for Income Taxes	$ 64	$ 46
Net Income	$ 124	$ 97

Growth Sales		5%
CGS as % of Sales	55%	53%
SG&A % of Sales	25%	30%
Taxrate	34%	32%

Impact of Changes in Selected Assumptions on Projected Income Statement

Colossal Chemical Corporation
Year Ended December 31, 2011
($000,000 omitted)

	Base Case	1% Increase in Gross Margin	1% Decline in Tax Rate	5% Increase in Sales
Sales	$2,110	$2,110	$2,110	$2,216
Cost of goods sold	1,477	1,456	1,477	1,551
Selling, general, and administrative expense	$ 253	$ 253	$ 253	$ 266
Depreciation	121	121	121	121
Research and development	84	84	84	84
Total costs and expenses	1,935	1,914	1,935	2,022
Operating Income	$ 175	$ 196	$ 175	$ 194
Interest expense	34	34	34	34
Interest (income)	(5)	(5)	(5)	(5)
Earnings before Income Taxes	$ 146	$ 167	$ 146	$ 165
Provision for Income Taxes	$ 50	$ 57	$ 48	$ 56
Net Income	$ 96	$ 110	$ 98	$ 109

Growth Sales	0%	0%	0%	5%
CGS as % of Sales	70%	69%	70%	70%
SG&A % of Sales	12%	12%	12%	12%
Taxrate	34%	34%	33%	34%

Impact of Changes in Selected Assumptions on Projected Income Statement

Colossal Chemical Corporation
Year Ended December 31, 2011
($000,000 omitted)

	Base Case	2% Increase in Gross Margin	2% Decline in Tax Rate	5% Increase in Sales
Sales	$2,110	$2,110	$2,110	$2,216
Cost of goods sold	1,477	1,350	1,393	1,462
Selling, general, and administrative expense	$ 253	$ 317	$ 317	$ 332
Depreciation	121	121	121	121
Research and development	84	84	84	84
Total costs and expenses	1,935	1,872	1,914	2,000
Operating Income	$ 175	$ 238	$ 196	$ 216
Interest expense	34	34	34	34
Interest (income)	(5)	(5)	(5)	(5)
Earnings before Income Taxes	$ 146	$ 209	$ 167	$ 187
Provision for Income Taxes	$ 50	$ 71	$ 53	$ 64
Net Income	$ 96	$ 138	$ 113	$ 123

Growth Sales	0%	0%	0%	5%
CGS as % of Sales	70%	64%	66%	66%
SG&A % of Sales	12%	15%	15%	15%
Taxrate	34%	34%	32%	34%

Impact of Changes in Selected Assumptions on Projected Income Statement

Colossal Chemical Corporation
Year Ended December 31, 2011
($000,000 omitted)

	Base Case	Forecast
Sales	$2,110	$2,216
Cost of goods sold	1,477	1,507
Selling, general, and administrative expense	$ 253	$ 377
Depreciation	121	121
Research and development	84	84
Total costs and expenses	1,935	2,088
Operating Income	$ 175	$ 127
Interest expense	34	34
Interest (income)	(5)	(5)
Earnings before Income Taxes	$ 146	$ 98
Provision for Income Taxes	$ 50	$ 31
Net Income	$ 96	$ 67
Growth Sales		5%
CGS as % of Sales	70%	68%
SG&A % of Sales	12%	17%
taxrate	34%	32%

CPSIA information can be obtained
at www.ICGtesting.com
Printed in the USA
LVHW082233300722
724806LV00015B/219

9 780470 640036